THE CRUCIFIXION COVER-UP

The untold story behind the trial, crucifixion and resurrection of Jesus the Christ

By
Burt Wilson

Copyright © July 2009
Burt Wilson/Paloria Press

TABLE OF CONTENTS

Forward..................................5

The Arrest and Trial of Jesus............11

Was Jesus the Messiah?...................50

The Crucifixion..........................58

The Resurrection.........................83

Epilogue: What was covered up?.......96

All Rights Reserved: No part of this publication may be reproduced, stored in a retrieval system, or transmitted in any form, by any means, electronic, mechanical, photo-copying, recording or otherwise, without permission in writing from the copyright owner or his representatives. Permission to quote freely given. Contact the publisher.

ISBN 978-0-578-03465-2

Other books by Burt Wilson:

Ancient Wisdom for the 21st Century
Available at www.lulu.com/burtwilson or amazon.com

The Leader (translation) by M. Roerich
Available at www.lulu.com/burtwilson

The Third Theory
Available by e-mail. Contact: bwilson5404@sbcglobal.net

Shakey & Me
Available by e-mail. Contact: bwilson5404@sbcglobal.net

A History of Sacramento Jazz
Available by e-mail. Contact: bwilson5404@sbcglobal.net

Complete Post Production with the Video Toaster
Out of print.

DEDICATION

To my beloved guru, friend and teacher

Ralph Harris Houston

FORWARD

Every once in awhile a Christian fanatic gets the idea that he wants to experience the suffering that Jesus endured on the cross, so he lies down semi-naked on a proper wooden cross and gets someone to nail the palms of his hands (or the wrists) and his feet to the beams. When the cross is stood up on its end, the person's body weight immediately tears his hands and feet loose and he slides ignominiously down to the ground.

Because this happened so frequently in the last century, people began to really wonder if the mode of crucifixion that has come down to us is different from what it was back then. Thus, in an effort to rationalize the familiar "nailed to the cross" traditional method, it was suggested in the 1960's that there was an outward-jutting "seat" fixed to the cross on which the victim's body was supported.

This soon fell out of favor, however, because it was felt that traditional Roman brutality, which was legendary, would never treat crucifixion so leniently. Researchers also said that such a method would prolong life for weeks when the whole idea was to get it over with in a few days. Not incidentally, it did not explain why the victim's legs had to be broken.

Then, in the 1970's a physician in Arizona came up with the idea that the hands were not only nailed to the cross, but ropes were used to bind the forearms to the horizontal beam. This satisfied the world that such a method would prevent a body from falling off the cross and everyone breathed a sigh of relief.

Furthermore, the doctor claimed that death came as a result of suffocation, i.e., it was the compression of the lungs that caused the person to slowly expire, producing a suffering, torturous demise. Still, why a victim's legs had to be broken, as the Bible relates, was a mystery.

This mystery is explained in this book. It is based on research done by French author Renée Dunan for his book on Julius Caesar (Re-titled for American consumption "The Love Life of Julius Caesar," (E. P. Dutton & Company, 1931). It demonstrates conclusively that the act of crucifixion had to include the practice of impalement. The actual procedure will be described in the section of this book that deals with Jesus' Crucifixion. As you will see, this is the only procedure that involves the breaking of legs—mystery solved!

The Roman spectacle of crucifixion by impalement was certainly meant to be as savagely and tortuously cruel as possible because it had to accomplish two things: 1) to act as a visual deterrent to crime, and 2) to provide a theater of gore to satisfy the blood lust of those who came to watch.

When it came to devising fiendish methods of torture and death, the Romans were without equal and every bloodthirsty method was utilized to its fullest extent. Hardy onlookers would show up at every crucifixion to watch the proceedings and even bring food with them so they would be sure not to miss the gory climax.

But the actual crucifixion process is only part of the story we will deal with here. There are also issues which have emerged which deal with historical accuracy, the hidden sacred subtext of the New Testament Gospels, the confusion between the man Jesus and the principle of the "Christ" and the difference between the two.

According to the Ancient Wisdom, the New Testament gospels are historically inaccurate because they actually conceal a hidden subtext that contains a Gnostic teaching of Initiation. This teaching, disguised in a historical narrative, concerns the path a person must take to attain "Christhood"—the union of one's individual consciousness with one's Divine Consciousness, the "God Within."

Thus, the candidate for Initiation serves and ministers to his fellow man, is consistently rebuffed by his own people and religious authorities and is metaphorically crucified by society at the intersection of the cross which symbolizes Spirit (the vertical beam) and Matter (the horizontal beam). The constant conflict that comes from serving ethereal Spirit in the midst of mundane Matter causes the candidate great suffering, but if the candidate persists, he will, at the end, have his spirit raised up to the point where he is anointed by the "Christ Principle." Thus he achieves his last Initiation–Mahatmaship.

It is important to become familiar with the fact that the Spiritual Principle the ancients called the "Christ" is actually the "*Christos*," (also "*Messiah*") a pre-Christian term meaning an anointing. The significance here is that the ancients believed a person could be *anointed* by the Christ Principle, but that no man could actually *be* a Christ. This is crucial to understanding how the biblical text of Jesus' trial was altered to make it appear he was *the* one-and-only Christ-in-the-flesh when such a possibility is a spiritual impossibility—totally illogical.

It was not until the Council of Nicea that Jesus was *voted* to be a consubstantial "Son of God," i.e., a "Christ-in-the-flesh." This was done to make of Jesus a *physical* God on earth and unique to early Catholicism so the church could provide a physical image of God—an idol, if you will—that would be more understandable to the masses who had no training in the abstracts of metaphysics.

As Mme. Blavatsky said, "The church carnalized Christ."

Finally, as any good student of the Bible knows, the Holy Scriptures have been changed, added to and rewritten to such an extent that the original beauty of the transcendental nature of Spirit has been brought down into a more mundane human form to make it easier to comprehend, i.e., easier to sell to the ignorant masses.

The three historical days that comprise the arrest, trial, crucifixion and so-called "resurrection" of Jesus are related here on three different levels concurrently. That is because the New Testament, i.e. the standard King James Version, was written on three levels as was the custom at the time by those who would preserve spiritual truth in myth and metaphor.

The first level, the level known only to strict Bible fundamentalists, is the written word as it stands alone. What you see and read is what you get: stark prose that tells a simple story in simple terms which, nevertheless, requires giant leaps of faith between belief and non-belief while challenging logic and understanding.

The second level is that which reveals the teachings of the Ancient Wisdom—such as Reincarnation and Karma and Jesus as a guru. Such concepts are not associated with the Bible or Jesus' teaching today because they were tossed out of the Church in 553 C.E. at a Conference of Cardinals in Constantinople when they declared anathema certain tracts authored by the learned Christian apologist Origen.

The third level is that of the path of Initiation to the principle of "Christhood." This is the most esoteric level of all because this is where the hidden subtext comes in. Thus where the Bible has Jesus saying, "I am the way, the truth and the life," it should rather be read as, "The Christ Principle is the way, the truth and the life."

All of the above levels will be dealt with concurrently as the narrative of the trial, crucifixion and resurrecttion unfolds. It follows Jesus' betrayal, his abandonment by all of his disciples, the brilliant non-defense which he uses to confuse Caiaphas, Pilate and Herod Antipas, his humiliation by the chief priests, the scribes and their mob of followers, the crucifixion and, for the want of a more precise term, the "resurrection."

An enhanced narrative is also woven into the standard Biblical account of events in order to supplement the stark prose of the story. It's meant to provide a more subjective level of thought and connectivity and explain more clearly the psychological battle that was going on between Jesus, his followers and his enemies. It also sheds light on Jesus' role as a guru (teacher) of the Ancient Wisdom.

By adding this supporting dialog and description, the story becomes more understandable and relevant in terms of the Ancient Wisdom. Although the additions are few, I have done this in the same manner as a motion picture writer would be compelled to write extra scenes in order to make a sparse story flow better so its content can be more fully understood.

Interspersed among the different levels are comments in darker text on the esoteric symbolism mentioned above which permeates the action. This level goes deeper into Jesus' life and how as a teacher he interrelates with his disciples. It takes Jesus' humanness, an aspect that is ignored in most other texts, and juxtaposes it with the literal narrative so that his human side can be better understood in a proper context. It is my belief that unless we understand Jesus as a human being first, we are not able to fully comprehend either his courage during his trial, his thought processes during his crucifixion or his very real spiritual achievements contained in his after-death appearances.

Finally, I do *not* believe that the Bible is the "Word of God" as the ecclesiastics do. I do believe that it is the "metaphor of God." I also believe that the Bible is a most sacred text which actually has more relevance to life today than it is given credit for—far beyond, in fact, any fundamentalist Christian's wildest dreams.

I view this work not as a re-write of the Bible, but as a "purification" of the ancient biblical texts. It is a task in which I have endeavored to release the allegorical Light that is embedded within these sacred texts. I hope that the rays of illumination that are released may pierce the darkness of centuries of dogmatic religious obfuscation and reveal the hidden truths therein.

Burt Wilson
Sacramento, CA
January 24, 2009

THE CRUCIFIXION COVER-UP

THE ARREST AND TRIAL OF JESUS

It was after the Passover Supper, just past midnight on Friday, when Jesus and his disciples entered the Garden of Gethsemane at the foot of the Mount of Olives. Stopping just inside the entrance to the grove, Jesus looked around the area and took a deep breath. The lingering odor of the olive presses came and went with the frequent gusts of wind that swept through the trees.

He turned and glanced at his disciples, quickly reading their faces. He saw in their eyes the look of expectation that he had by now become used to. Because he was their guru and leader and they trusted him, they had placed their spiritual lives in his hands. They expected all manner of leadership from him, thus he could show no fear lest he lose their conviction in the purpose of his mission. Nevertheless, like any human being, he was having doubts.

The disciples, too, were on emotional overload. Jesus had just told them not once but quite a few times that one of them would betray him this morning. Each of them had asked, "Master, is it I?" but Jesus would say nothing more than "The one who does it will wish that he had never been born." But for now the cool spring night provided welcome relief from the hot desert sun and all the disciples were eager to take the usual after-dinner walk with their leader. Jesus could clairvoyantly see and feel their tension.

Jesus was a guru and as all gurus, he had disciples. They addressed him usually as "Master," not in the manner of a master-slave relationship, but because at Jesus' high level of Initiation into the "Mysteries" (He entered schools of wisdom in Greece and India and took Egyptian initiations in the Great Pyramid of Cheops during his so-called "lost years"), he had become a "Master of Spirit," i.e. one who had mastered his lower nature and was now operating continually on a very high spiritual level with the attendant powers of clairvoyance and clairaudience. Possessing such power, Jesus could read the thoughts of his disciples and, in fact, anyone who approached him, but as with all High Initiates, he could never use that power to physically save himself from harm.

The betrayal of one's guru is considered the most heinous act for a disciple. That's because betrayal is a well-thought-out, premeditated action and for it to take place the betrayer must have first been accepted by the guru into the circle of disciples. Although some disciples may betray out of ignorance—which is dealt with on another level--a conscious betrayal is the worst of all spiritual offences. The Russian metaphysician, Mme. Helena Roerich, writes that, "Betrayal, like a shadow, follows a great achievement, and precisely by betrayal the greatness of an achievement can be measured." In the Esoteric Doctrine of the Ancient Wisdom, betrayal is always prelude to spiritual success. Had not Judas betrayed Jesus, for example, Jesus' real mission on earth would have been lost in history. The Ancient Wisdom says we all have our future betrayer which will signal our approach to "Christhood."

James spoke first. "Why don't you tell us which one is going to betray you, Master?" he asked.

"Because all of you will find reason enough this night to betray me," Jesus answered. "But don't worry about that too much because I'll be with you in Galilee when it's all over. There, you will see me again almost as I am now."

Peter immediately jumped up and said, "Even though the rest of the disciples may find a reason to betray you, I certainly will not."

Jesus smiled. "My dear friend Peter," he said, "before this night is over you will betray me, not once, but three times before the first rooster crows."

Peter protested vehemently. "Even if I would be crucified with you I would not betray you," he said. And all the disciples looked at each other and nodded their heads, affirming their own feelings that they would never be a party to the betrayal of their teacher.

Jesus held up his hand and the disciples ceased talking amongst themselves. "I need some time to meditate and think some things through," he said, "so I want you all to stay here and wait for me while I go up to that tree on the side of the hill and rest awhile. Don't worry. I'll take Peter and James and John with me to look out for any danger." There were a few protests from the rest of the disciples, but they all did as he said.

Moving along the side of the hill, Jesus suddenly felt faint and grabbed James' arm.

"Make sure I don't fall," he said to James. James put his arm around Jesus just the way many of the disciples loved to do as a friendly gesture. He held him tightly, supporting him by holding him snugly against his side. The disciples did not appear to notice anything unusual as it looked to them like a routine gesture. "Is there something we can do," James whispered?

All gurus, while they never show partiality to their disciples, nevertheless have an "inner circle" of disciples with whom they are more simpatico. Peter, James and John were the ones Jesus felt more comfortable with when he needed human support and this was a night when he needed it badly. One would think that this would cause dissension in a group of disciples, and to a certain extent it did, but the Esoteric Doctrine of the Ancient Wisdom always considered this a test of discipleship. If one took offense at being supposedly "left out" of some real or imagined "inner" group, it showed he was not grateful for just being "in" the circle of a guru's disciples–which should be enough for anyone.

"Just...stay...with me," Jesus stammered. His breathing was heavy, but he fought back the feeling of nausea and composed himself. "Up until now," he went on, "even though I've known most of my life that my mission would end in this way, it's always been to me something abstract and in the future. Now that it's here, I wonder if I can go through with it."

Peter, James and John had never heard such talk from Jesus before. Jesus saw their confused looks and said, "It's hard to describe. I'm not even sure if I'm prepared for it. Working through the circumstances whereby I will come to be crucified is one thing. Actually suffering it is another."

At this, Peter, James and John stopped. James again asked, "What can we do? There must be something we can do?" Jesus looked at them one by one. "Just...be my friend for a moment," he said. "Just stay with me. I can already feel around me the dark vibrations—the evil energies that are behind what is to come. They crisscross in the atmosphere and reinforce each other. The air is heavy with evil. It's so strong I can almost touch it. It's like I'm being ground into the earth by a huge boulder. Do me a favor and wait here for me. I'm going on around the side of hill to be by myself for awhile."

Jesus left the three disciples and walked on along the path. Every step was a struggle and when he was out of sight and the darkness had closed in behind him he fell to the ground, his fingers digging into the soft earth.

"Master!" Jesus cried out, appealing to his guru while trying to stifle the word as soon as he said it. "I don't know if I have the strength to go through with this. I pray that if it is possible that this cup of poison be lifted from me. If there is any way my mission can be fulfilled without my being crucified, please, *please* let me know. I need to know. Now!"

The "Cup of Poison" Jesus mentioned is the karmic glyph from a negative act from some past incarnation that must be worked out in a future life. In Jesus' case it had to be fulfilled through the act of crucifixion. This is also the meaning of the idea that the Law of Karma seeks restitution until "every jot and tittle" (the smallest measures known in biblical times) is removed. Jesus was undoubtedly wondering aloud if the positive things he had done in this line could serve as recompense for the negative glyph from a past life. Karma is, however, inexorable. It

was Mme. Helena P. Blavatsky who wrote that if we were able to look inside the Akashic Records we would surely find that in some far distant past life of the man who is now Jesus we would find the cause of his crucifixion in this life.

Jesus' chest heaved against the ground as he sobbed out the last few words. He cried uncontrollably for a few minutes, moving his head from side to side. Tears rolled down his cheeks and fell to the ground. Then he abruptly stopped crying. Lifting himself up by his hands and turning over, he came up into a sitting position, his head down and his arms hanging loosely between his legs. After a moment he looked up. "OK," he said to himself, brushing off his tunic, "I know. This is my mission and I'm here to fulfill your will, not mine." After a few more minutes he got up and walked back to join Peter, James and John.

When he came upon the three disciples he found them all asleep. He kicked Peter gently and woke him up. Peter awakened with a start and rubbed his eyes. Seeing Jesus he said, "Master, you're back already?"

"It's been an hour," Jesus said angrily. "What's the matter with all of you? Couldn't you stay awake even one hour for my sake?" The disciples were not used to being chastised in such a manner. They immediately began to believe that what they were about to experience was serious business. "You had all better stay awake and meditate," Jesus said. "I suggest that you concentrate on the power to resist temptation because as far as I can see the spirit may be willing, but the flesh is weak."

In using the phrase "the flesh is weak," Jesus was giving his disciples an advance warning that a big test was in the offing for all of them. For the person following the path of discipleship that path has, since time immemorial, always been a path of tests. A disciple is constantly tested as to his ability to control his thoughts and emotions in order to perceive and penetrate the whirl of events going on around him. The Samurai warrior and martial arts systems use this same principle. Jesus had instructed his disciples for years in the reality of the spiritual universe as opposed to the illusions of the earthly world. But such lessons usually remain only abstracts to the disciple until the hour of trial comes.

Jesus backed away a few steps and then abruptly turned his back on the three disciples and returned to the spot where he had been before. He felt as alone as one could be. After a few minutes he fell to his knees and prayed: "Oh Master, if this is truly my karma and there is no other way for it to be discharged except by me, so be it. May thy will be done."

After awhile, Jesus returned to Peter, James and John who were again fast asleep. He didn't even try to wake them, but returned again to the same place along the side of the hill. He knelt down and prayed "Master, I still ask that if my mission can be accomplished without my being crucified, please let it be." He meditated a long time. When he finished the dawn was just beginning to cast an eerie half-light on the shaded side of the hill. Jesus rose up and said softly, "Thank you. I understand completely now why it can't be any other way."

Returning to his three disciples for the third time, Jesus found them still asleep. He gazed upon them for a moment and then spoke in a low voice: "So you're still sleeping. Well, you're going to need your rest because the hour has come when I will be betrayed." Walking to the other side of the sleeping group he saw that the larger band of disciples further away was also asleep, so he raised his voice to a pitch where all could hear him and shouted, "Awake! Awake! It's time to go. My betrayer is just entering the garden. We must go to meet him."

While Jesus was waking up his disciples, Judas appeared at the gates of the garden along with a band of soldiers and some officers of the chief priests and the Pharisees. They were carrying lanterns and torches and the soldiers had weapons. Judas sidled up to the commander of the band and said, "Watch me. I will kiss the man you want. Seize him and lead him away, but be sure he is under a secure guard." Then Judas walked out from the band of soldiers and went immediately up to Jesus. "Hail, Master," he said in greeting and kissed Jesus on the cheek, the usual sign of love and respect of a disciple for his guru.

It may well have been that Judas actually approached Jesus and kissed him as a sign of recognition for the guard commander. On the other hand, he could have easily just pointed him out. Certainly the chief priests and the Pharisees knew Jesus by sight. Nevertheless, "the kiss of betrayal" (forever known after this incident as the "Judas Kiss.") has long been a part of the Esoteric Doctrine and a big factor in the guru-disciple relationship. The

disciple always greets the guru with a kiss—usually on both cheeks. Thus the guru can tell instantly what's going on in the heart of a disciple by the quality of his kiss. There is no mistaking it because there is no such thing as deceiving the guru. Thus by having Judas kiss Jesus, the writer of the gospel--who was probably conversant with the Esoteric Doctrine-- was using a symbol which would only be recognized by a reader also familiar with that doctrine.

In a larger context, the sacred law of Initiation has it that the final Initiation, that which Jesus is about to undergo, is always—*always*—preceded by an act of betrayal by a friend. Judas, then, is the betrayer that assures Jesus of his final Initiation. Many people not familiar with this law have tried to put forward the idea that Judas did him a favor and that was his *duty* in this life; that he was predestined to play that role. Not so. We all have a choice as to our actions in life and that is what Free Will is all about.

Jesus, who clairvoyantly knew what Judas was up to, nevertheless said, "Friend, why are you here?" But before Judas could answer, the soldiers surrounded the group of disciples and began taking them into custody. Three of the biggest soldiers burst through the resulting melee and seized Jesus by both arms. The other soldiers began encircling the rest of the disciples.

"Wait!" Jesus shouted. His voice was so loud and commanding that all stopped in their tracks. Looking directly at the commander of the guard and the chief priests and Pharisees, Jesus looked them in the eye and asked, "Whom do you seek?"

"Jesus of Nazareth," the commander answered.

"I am he," Jesus answered. There was such power in his voice that those soldiers nearest him, along with Judas, fell backwards onto the ground.

The commander and a few of his men advanced toward Jesus, but after a few steps, Peter drew his short sword and swung it against the head of Malchus, one of the slaves of the high priest. The blade made a sweeping upward and downward arc, smacking Malchus on the left side of his head and, continuing downwards, cleanly lopped off his ear.

Jesus grabbed Peter and shoved him away. "No more of this," he said. "Sheath your sword!" Then he quickly cupped his hand around the soldier's bleeding ear and held it there, focusing his energy on it for a few seconds. When he drew his hand away, his healing powers had not only stopped the bleeding, but had completely restored the severed ear to its former condition.

Jesus then turned around and focused his gaze again on the commander. "I said, whom do you seek?" he repeated.

Again the commander shouted out, "Jesus of Nazareth!"

Jesus looked the commander up and down and walked toward him, gesturing at all the weaponry and armor he was carrying. "You look more like you're out after a thief with all your swords and clubs," he said. "I told you that I am he. Therefore if you seek me, then let the rest of these men go."

The commander nodded to his men. Jesus' disciples did not even wait to see what was going to happen to their guru. As one man they turned and fled every which way, causing much confusion all around. The soldiers began to give chase but all they were able to do was grab the linen wrap with which a young man was clothed. The man escaped by slipping out of his clothes and continued, running, naked, with the rest. Thus Jesus was left alone, forsaken by every one of his disciples. The commander was afraid that Jesus might also escape, but since he was the one they were really after, he quickly regrouped his soldiers and, binding Jesus' hands, took him into custody.

And so the "flesh" *was* "weak," just as Jesus had predicted. Since discipleship is a period of alternately learning the Esoteric Doctrine and then putting that doctrine into practice, this would be an important lesson in the training of each disciple. The fact that they had let down their guru in his hour of need would haunt them the rest of their lives, indeed for many lifetimes to come. This lesson would be indelibly imprinted in the forefront of their minds so in future lives they might make the right decision in similar circumstances.

It was also a demonstration to them of Jesus' own commitment to the esoteric doctrine he preached. Thus he confirmed with decisive action his own teaching (John 15:13) that "Greater love hath no man than this, that a man lay down his life for his friends." This is exactly what Jesus did for his disciples. He actively confirmed his teaching and his love for them on this cold, damp spring morning. Thus was the real power of Jesus' teaching   clearly demonstrated to all the disciples.

The guard immediately took Jesus to the Sanhedrin where all the scribes, Chief Priests and elders had gathered and placed him before the high priest, Caiaphas. Peter had followed the guard to the Sanhedrin and watched them go inside. He saw Judas also join them inside. Because Peter was known to be a disciple of Jesus and easily recognized by his huge build, he cautiously waited outside the door. But Judas, seeing Peter by the door, went to him and invited him in. Peter looked around and began to pass through the door, but the servant who was guarding the door recognized him. "Aren't you one of Jesus' disciples?" the servant asked.

"No, I am not," said Peter and passed through the door.

Inside, the servants and officers of the guard had made a fire to warm them against the early morning chill. Peter went and stood with them, holding his hands out to catch the warmth of the coals. One of the officers looked at Peter and said, "Isn't this man also one of Jesus' disciples?"

Peter, seeking to immediately end the conversation before it got out of hand, denied the accusation most vehemently. "I am *not*," he said.

But the brother of the soldier whose ear Peter had cut off stared long and hard at the big fisherman. "Didn't I see you in the garden with him?" he asked.

Peter stiffened. "No, no, *no!*" he said loudly. "I don't even know what you are talking about!" At that, Jesus turned around and looked at Peter and immediately the rooster crowed.

Caiaphas stood by quietly while the soldiers blindfolded Jesus. When the blindfold was in place and tied securely, they spit on him and beat him, saying: "You call yourself a prophet. Well let's see you prophesy who hit you!"

Caiaphas, wanting to get on with the business of finding Jesus guilty of treason, stopped the soldiers from beating Jesus and called for order. Stepping into the center of the room, commanding attention, he said, "We are here this morning to hear your complaints against this man." The room grew ever more silent. "I invite you now to come forward with your testimony so we can quickly conclude this matter."

Many of the people present went before Caiaphas and told him their reasons why Jesus should be tried as a traitor. The testimony of two of them was that Jesus had said that he was able to destroy the temple of God and re-build it in three days." "He would tear down our most sacred place," one man said. "That is truly treasonous."

The other man said, "He told how he would destroy this temple made with hands and in three days build another not made with hands."

This testimony against Jesus probably came from a spy who had stood at the fringes of groups of people who listened to Jesus imparting the Esoteric Doctrine to his disciples. In the Ancient Wisdom, the "temple" is a metaphor for one's body. It's used many times in the New Testament. A more complete explanation is that "the body is the temple of the Spirit." This is very meaningful because the doctrine says that unless the body is kept as pure as a temple, the disciple will be unable to make any spiritual advancement. Most harmful to the body, however, are "unclean" thoughts, narcotics (especially those that attack the central nervous system) and over indulgence in the material aspects of life, i.e. lust, greed, power, control, etc. The whole idea is that the

"spiritual path" which leads to redemption and enlightenment is one of the refinement of the spirit and the spirit cannot be refined in an unclean vessel.

Judaic Law is based upon this same principle (sometimes carried too far as always happens when religions evolve hundreds of years beyond their original doctrine). It is believed that following certain rules of cleanliness keeps the "temple" purified and thus makes it easier for a person to receive "insight," as it were, into the metaphysical aspects of life. As in so many different religions, however, the spirit of the law becomes lost, obliterated in the repetition of the letter of the law.

In ancient alchemy, it was believed that the "Philosopher's Stone" was able to bring about the transmutation of base metal into gold. Of course, this is a metaphor for the transmutation of one's base life (metal=material) into the spiritual life (gold=God) and the Philosopher's Stone that facilitates this is actually the application of one's knowledge of the Esoteric Doctrine to daily life. The Philosopher's Stone (an oxymoron designed to mislead the profane) is really not a stone, but the Book of Knowledge of the Ancient Wisdom.

The fact that a man said, "He would destroy this temple made with hands and in three days build another not made with hands" needs explaining. What Jesus was actually telling his disciples was the manner in which he would appear to them after his death–that he would appear not in a physical body, but in an invisible "astral" body. When he used the phrase that it could not be "made with the hands" he was using a metaphor for the fact that his final

Initiation would give him the power to both disintegrate and re-integrate the atoms of his physical body. Thus he would be able to build a new "spiritual," i.e., ethereal body, within three days of the death of his "temple"–his physical body. This is the manner in which he was able to appear to his disciples after death.

Caiaphas, a bright man with a legal mind, knew that the chief priests had put these people up to testifying against Jesus, but he also saw that the testimony of these two would not hold up because it was too conflicting. Therefore he decided to use a lawyer's trick—making Jesus at least deny that he had said what he was accused of. He could then get Jesus on making a false statement.

"Well," he said, turning to Jesus, "do you have any statement to make about this? Do these men speak the truth about you?" Jesus clairvoyantly knew what Caiaphas was up to so he did not answer. He knew that silence could not be used against him, but if he spoke, even using his clairvoyance, he could fall into one of the verbal traps Caiaphas was trying to lead him into, so he looked down at the ground and spoke not a word.

With Jesus' prolonged silence, Caiaphas could see that his task was not going to be an easy one. He quickly decided to ask Jesus a series of questions that Jesus could easily answer, hoping Jesus would inadvertently say something that would be contradictory and provide grounds for a trial. He smiled at Jesus and asked, "Well then, tell me something about your disciples and your teaching. I'm not familiar with it."

"You should be," Jesus answered. "I have taught openly everywhere. I have always taught in synagogues and in the temple where all Jews come together. I have said nothing secretly. So I don't understand why you're asking me this question. If you want to know about my teaching, ask those who have heard me. They know what I have said."

At this, one of the officers gave Jesus a blow to the head and said, "Is this how you answer a high priest?"

"If I have spoken wrongly, bear witness to the wrong; but if I have spoke rightly, why do you strike me?" Jesus answered.

Caiaphas now knew that none of the usual tactics was going to trick Jesus into any kind of testimony that could be used against him. He could also see that Jesus was bound to tell the truth, but was smart enough to do so in a way that would not incriminate himself. So the cunning Caiaphas decided to turn Jesus' tactic against him. "I would like to know if you are indeed the Christ. If you are, tell us."

It is extremely doubtful that Caiaphas actually asked Jesus if he were a "Christ." The charges against Jesus, indeed the pivotal point of the whole trial, was whether he was claiming he was the "King of the Jews." It's more likely Caiaphas asked Jesus if he were the "Messiah." That would have made more sense in these proceedings.

Are we saying that Bible Scripture was altered? Yes. The Greek word for "Christ" is "Christos" and it also means "Messiah." Since the church under the Emperor Constantine was intent in making of Jesus a bodily "Christ," the good fathers probably changed the operative word from "Messiah" to "Christ" to suit their own purposes. Proof is in the fact that Jesus

as a "Christ" had nothing to do with being the "King of the Jews" and the Jewish concept of the "Messiah" had everything to do with it. It is well to consider that bible scholars have in the last 100 years counted some 50,000 changes, deletions and errors that have been found in the Holy Scriptures.

Why do we suspect the scriptures were altered here? Because it was not until a conference of bishops at Nicea in 325 C.E. that Jesus was actually *voted* to be a "Son of God," thus a "Christ"—by the Roman Catholic Church.

At that time the Church took the Gnostic idea of the "Christos"—a *High Spiritual Principle* from which the word "Christ" is derived—and applied it to Jesus as a *bodily principle* to make of him a living "Son of God" on earth. In other words, the Catholic Church manufactured a "Christ-in-the-flesh" in order to persuade people that God actually walked on earth as Jesus and that this is what made the Catholic religion different and truer from all others.

This declaration also presented Jesus as an idol to people for worship. Because the masses were so uneducated, they couldn't understand such abstracts as spiritual "principles," so this move gave people a more human and "realizable" personal God vs. the distant "Sun-as-God" the Pagans worshiped.

This was all done at the request of the Emperor Constantine because it was his plan to use the church as an arm of control of the Roman Empire. He was pleased that the Catholic religion preached such things as "the meek will inherit the earth" and "love your enemies" and he saw in these religious messages a docile religion that would not foment rebellion.

There were two similar phrases in use in that era and unless one is versed in the religious language of those days, they can be very confusing. The two words are "Chrestos" and "Christos." Chrestos is a Gnostic term. If a person was called a "Chrestos" it meant that he/she was simply "a good person," i.e., he/she helped others and was a true spiritual worker. Thus, being a Chrestos meant that one was "on the path" to God Consciousness. In the temples of Egypt a neophyte was called a "Chrestos." Interestingly enough, the word that was used for a group of people or neophytes following a spiritual path was the plural "Chrestians."

"Christos" is different from "Chrestos." It is "basically a Greek term from Athenian times and signifies a person anointed by the "Christ Principle." Such a Christ is never considered to be a person. In other words, in the ancient Mystery Schools, the struggling and suffering neophyte was a Chrestos while on the path, but that path led ultimately to the Supreme Goal: the anointing, or overshadowing, of the neophyte by the Christos. This is the same thing as having attained God Consciousness. When this happened, the neophyte became a "purified Christ," i.e., one able to perceive cosmic truth and act as a Messenger of Spiritual Wisdom to others.

Thus the bottom line is that no person, then or now, can ever actually *become* a Christ, *per se*. One can come to be under the influence or be "anointed" (which is a kind of overshadowing) by the Spiritual Principle of the Christ, but can never actually *be* one in flesh and blood. It can be pictured as raising one's consciousness to contact the highest level of wisdom.

Paul confirmed this when he wrote (1 Corinthians 15:50), "Now this I say, brethren, that flesh and blood cannot inherit the kingdom of God." This is pretty clear!

Thus the church mutilated this sacred concept beyond all recognition by devising Jesus as a "Christ-in-the flesh"—an ugly distortion of the metaphysical truth—and then forced this concept on worshipers by arbitrary decree. Thus the idea of Jesus ever being a "Christ-in-the-flesh" is nothing but church propaganda and not true.

The church fathers were also aware that a lie, if big enough and adhered to steadily, would, after three generations, become the *Catholica Veritus*—the Catholic truth. And so it did.

This makes it clear that what Caiaphas was really asking Jesus was whether he was indeed the Messiah.

Jesus looked Caiaphas squarely in the eye and said, "If I were to tell you that I am, you would not believe me. And if I were to ask you the same question, you wouldn't answer either."

According to the Esoteric Doctrine of the Ancient Wisdom, a very strict condition of that doctrine is that no one who has been anointed by the Christ Principle is allowed to actually *proclaim* his own anointing to others. This would be the biggest ego trip of the ages! Anyone who did this would expose himself right off as unworthy of such an anointing and at the very least a spiritual imposter. It simply isn't done. So in this exchange, Jesus was actually challenging Caiaphas' credentials as a priest.

Caiaphas, who was obviously learned in the mysteries, knew this. And he also must have known Jesus' teaching as his spies reported everything Jesus said and did to him. Although Jesus had done nothing wrong, all the priests of the Sanhedrin were worried over what Jesus was teaching to the people because he was, from time to time, disclosing the innermost esoteric tenets of Judaic theology and actually suggesting new understandings of ancient principles, especially such aspects as the Law of Karma, the inner meaning of which enabled one to achieve God Consciousness on his own with no need of any priesthood.

Caiaphas knew that if Jesus were overshadowed by the Christ Principle, i.e., that if he *really was* a Christ, he would not be able to admit to it. By the same token, Jesus knew that Caiaphas, although his ego wanted people to think that he might be overshadowed by the Christ Principle or else think that he himself just might be of Messiah material, was *not* overshadowed by either and to actually indicate as much–*by either a "yes" or "no"*--would be tantamount to an admission that he was neither.

And so we have this delicious little cat-and-mouse game going on between Jesus—the one who was really anointed by the Christ Principle—and the High Priest Caiaphas, who was extremely envious because he was not.

Caiaphas did his best to conceal his rage. He knew that people were referring to Jesus as a Christ, but he, the High Priest of the Sanhedrin, had never even been thought of in this manner, primarily because he wasn't a healer–which a true Christ would probably be. Jesus' answer now turned the focus of the question back on him and directly called his spiritual worthiness as a High Priest into question before the assembly. Caiaphas, moving around Jesus, thought a minute and then decided to ask the same question in a different way. "Tell us," he said, extending his arms palms up, thus including the whole assembly with him, "are you a son of God?"

Jesus was silent for a moment. Then he answered: "So sayest thou."

Here we have the use of the phrase "son of God" supposedly coming out of the mouth of Caiaphas. This is direct proof that the Bible was tampered with during the many "revisions" it went through from the moment of its canonization in 325 C.E. Here's why: Biblical scholars put the date that the four Gospels of the New Testament were written as between 80 and 100 C.E. Therefore one must ask why a phrase being used to describe an incident that happened in 33 C.E. was not even a part of Roman Catholic doctrine until the year 325 C.E.?

The answer is, again, that the church wanted to see this in the scriptures so it would give a kind of backdated authority to the concept of Jesus as the Son of God. This would make it look as if Jesus' contemporaries, mainly his disciples, were referring to him as such in the days that he walked the earth. The Bible is full of such "doctoring" and for one to think that the learned fathers were above such a thing is to be ignorant of early Christian history.

Again, what Caiaphas was probably really asking is, "Are you the Messiah?" This is more than likely

because Jesus' command of the workings of Judaic Law was so precise that he was a very real threat to Caiaphas' authority as a high priest. He obviously made Caiaphas feel very insecure.

Jesus' answer was brilliant because, "so sayest thou," is the equivalent today of saying, "You said it, I didn't."

Unfortunately, this very equivocal statement by Jesus has been used by the church as proof of his admission of his Godly status. Actually, no such thing would ever come forth from the mouth of one who was anointed by the Christ Principle. It would be considered a statement of personal ego and therefore a mis-use of spiritual standing. In truth, Jesus didn't really admit anything, but he very cleverly directed the accusation right back at Caiaphas.

Caiaphas' eyebrows narrowed. He now had what he wanted–a response that could easily be twisted in his favor. He knew the rabble in attendance was emotionally charged up and would only hear what they wanted to hear anyway, so he jumped up and down, took off his robe and tore it into two pieces in order to make sure he had everyone's attention and screamed, "Did you hear him? Did you hear him say so? He has made blasphemy against the Lord God. What further testimony do you need than this? We have heard it ourselves from his own lips!"

With that, the soldiers began again to beat Jesus, loudly repeating, "If you are a Christ, prophesy which of us just struck you!" Now Caiaphas felt he had enough to take Jesus before Pontius Pilate at the praetorium, the palace of the Roman governor.

Outside in the street, the mob pushed and shoved the exhausted Jesus all the way to the praetorium. When they arrived, they placed him in the center of a huge room and called for the Roman governor to come and see what they had brought to him. Pilate heard all the commotion and left his living quarters and entered the room. Exuding regal bearing, he moved slowly, looking around the hall at the crowd that had gathered there. When he knew he had their attention he halted and said, "What is this man charged with? Who is accusing him of what?"

"If this man had done nothing wrong would we have brought him here to hand over to you?" said one of the scribes, sarcastically.

Pilate smiled. He knew what they were up to. They wanted him to do their dirty-work for them. "Take him yourselves and judge him by your own law," he said, turning around to leave the room.

"It is not lawful for us to put any man to death," said one of the scribes. "We have found this man to be a traitor, undermining the sacred religion of our nation and forbidding us to give tribute to Caesar. And as if that were not enough, he had the gall to give testimony that he himself was a Christ--a King!"

Again, the original gospel manuscript most likely read "...to call himself a Messiah–a King!" Common sense tells us that the accusers were not looking for a Christ, but rather looking for a Messiah and that is why Jesus was often referred to by the people as the long-awaited "King of the Jews." Now they are laying the groundwork for the charge of sedition, a charge that would interest Pilate.

The latter remark caused Pilate to turn around and re-enter the hall. He stood for a moment looking at Jesus and then walked up to him and asked: "Do *you* claim to be the King of the Jews?"

A lightning change in the fundamental charges against Jesus occurs here. It is evident that the Chief Priests, scribes and Pharisees have concocted yet a different scheme of offences to use before Pilate, one that is more political than the religious argument they used on Caiaphas.
Since the Jewish Messiah was predicted to be a king and Jesus was hailed as a king who was teaching in the land of Judea, Jesus was everywhere talked about as the long-awaited Messiah—he who would lead the Jewish people out of bondage. From whose bondage? Rome's of course.
But whereas Caiaphas was worried about spiritual competition, Pilate was worried about political competition, so the priests of the Sanhedrin now smartly positioned Jesus as a threat to Roman order, a charge guaranteed to get Pilate's attention. Thus they repeated the false accusations against Jesus, saying that he was the "King of the Jews"–the Messiah. And it worked.

Jesus knew where this new charge came from. He lifted his head and gazed at Pilate. "Do you say this of your own accord, or did others prompt you beforehand to say such a thing?"

Pilate folded his tunic and came still nearer to Jesus and, in a low voice, said, "Am I a Jew?" There was a snide, half-laugh in his voice. "*I* don't need to be put up to anything. It is *your* own nation and its chief priests who have handed *you* over to *me*. Have you not heard their testimony against you?" Then Pilate raised his voice to Jesus so all could hear him. "Why don't you answer the charges?"

Jesus' answer was to remain silent. Pilate was now determined to hear Jesus answer at least one question so he asked him: "Where are you from?"

But Jesus continued his silence.

Pilate then circled around him, staring at him, finally stopping in front of him again. "You don't want to speak to me? Don't you know that I have the power to either release you or crucify you?"

Jesus gazed steadily at him and said, "The only power you have over me is what *I* give you. And regardless of what *you* choose to do, it will be those who delivered me to you who will have the greater sin."

This short speech has a great deal of esoteric importance. When he says, "The only power you have over me is what I give you," Jesus is asserting his independence from temporal law.

In *The Power of Myth*, Joseph Campbell writes about a person who is "...living not in terms of himself but in terms of an imposed system." He says, "This is the threat to our lives that we all face today. Is the system going to flatten you out and deny you your humanity, or are you going to be able to make use of the system to the attainment of human purposes? How do you relate to the system so that you are not compulsively serving it? How to do it? By holding to your own ideals for yourself and rejecting the system's impersonal claims upon you."

Jesus' words caused pandemonium among all the accusers. But Jesus still remained silent, not answering or saying anything. Pilate again held out his hands, palms up, and said to the assembled throng, "I can find no crime in him." Then he turned to leave the room.

This further incensed the crowd. Then a Pharisee yelled out over the rest, "He stirs up the people and teaches throughout all Judea from Galilee even to this city." This is proof that certain "plants" in the room had ready-made retorts for all possibilities.

When Pilate heard these words he froze. He thought that if Jesus were indeed a Galilean he then belonged to Herod Antipas' jurisdiction and it would thus be he who would decide Jesus' fate. So Pilate immediately ordered his guard to take Jesus to Herod's house. Much of the crowd which had been at the praetorium went along too because they were curious to see what would happen.

Herod Antipas (son of King Herod) was actually pleased to see Jesus. He had heard about him for quite some time and hoped to see some miracle or phenomena performed by him. When the two met, Herod questioned Jesus at length, just as Pilate had done, and Jesus, as he did before with Pilate, remained silent.

The Chief Priests and scribes who were closely following the action vehemently accused Jesus of every crime they could think of, but Jesus still gave no answer.

Herod Antipas quickly grew weary of questioning Jesus and decided to chastise Jesus with a show of contempt. He had the soldiers of his guard dress Jesus in gorgeous red robes, as if he were a king, while they mocked him continuously. After they had their fun for awhile they removed all the clothing from Jesus and sent him back to Pilate.

Pilate could hear the mob coming back to the praetorium and he guessed the worst. He was now desperate to figure a way out of this so when the crowd arrived he called the Chief Priests and the mob leaders into a private session. "You brought me this man as one who was perverting the people," he lectured them sternly, "and after examining him before you, I could not find this man guilty of any of the charges you made against him. Neither did Herod and, as you can see, he sent him back to me. I tell you right now that nothing deserving of death has been done by him, therefore I am going to chastise him and then release him."

The leaders from the Sanhedrin immediately huddled together and talked quietly among themselves, discussing what to do next. Pilate seemed to know what they were doing and gave them time to figure out a new accusation. Finally, one of the Jewish scribes yelled out so loudly that all in the hall could hear, "If you release him it will prove that you are not a friend of Caesar's. This man not only tells us we don't have to pay tribute to Caesar but by the very act of calling himself the King of the Jews he sets himself directly against Caesar." The crowd went wild at hearing this new accusation and repeated their calls for Jesus' crucifixion.

When Pilate heard these words he knew that he was now walking a razor's edge. If he released Jesus, the scribes and Pharisees would make sure that word got back to Emperor Tiberius that he appeased an enemy of Rome. Caiaphas would see to that. But if he crucified Jesus, he would be open to criticism from Jesus' own followers that he put to death an innocent man without any proof. This too would probably cause all kinds of civil unrest because Jesus' followers were numerous and could make quite a public ruckus. If that got back to Rome, as it surely would, the effect would be the same.

Pilate thought that his only chance was to make Jesus appear to be guilty but to place the responsibility for that guilt on the Jews. After all, hadn't Jesus indicated to him that they bore the greater sin. He knew that he had to do something that would show that the Jews, and not him, were the one's responsible for Jesus' crucifixion. With this plan in mind, he went and sat down on the seat of judgment. The crowd grew quiet because this meant that a decision was forthcoming.

Pilate sat thinking for a moment, letting the rabble see he was deliberating. Then he stood up moved back into the center of the room and, motioned dramatically toward Jesus. Then, using a sweeping gesture to include everyone present, he shouted, "Behold your king!"

The crowd immediately burst into cries of, "Take him away! Take him away and crucify him!"

Pilate smiled, aware that his theatrics had accomplished what he wanted. "What?" he said to the crowd. "Shall I crucify your king?"

The Chief Priests and the assembled rabble answered back as one voice, "We have no king but Caesar!" The rest of the multitude screamed their approval.

Pilate thought he had them now. But the crowd immediately moved closer to Pilate and, at the direction of one of the Chief Priests, began chanting, "Release Barabbas." They did this because it was a custom at this feast time to have a prisoner released and given his freedom. Rome thought that such a gesture would project a more compassionate image in its Jewish provinces. Thus it was the custom for the people to make the selection. Among the rebels in prison was a man called Barabbas who had committed murder in a past insurrection. Prompted by the Chief Priests, the crowd now chose Barabbas and was making its choice known to Pilate. Of course, this was a previously-planned tactic in order to preempt Pilate from choosing Jesus to be the one released.

A reading of the scriptures makes it clear that the Chief Priests, Scribes and Pharisees had a strategy for every event that night, even for their case to be heard before Herod if the trial before Pilate didn't go according to plan. Every step appears to have been orchestrated to achieve a decision in their favor. Everything smacks of premeditation and collusion between the Jewish priests and the Elders who controlled the mob. They visibly wanted to–were bound to—somehow evoke a death sentence for Jesus. And we can be sure that Caiaphas and the Chief Priests and Scribes put them up to it.

It is clear that these scriptures present us with a Jesus who is a religious radical in the strictest sense; one who seeks to go to the roots of a religion to examine its truths in order to shock its present day adherents into seeing how corrupted it has become.

In fact, this happens to most all religions over time. As Mme. H. P. Blavatsky writes, "all religions are true on the bottom and false on top." This can't be avoided because political and social changes cause the original religious doctrines to be amended and modified and thus lose their real meaning. Jesus was simply trying to bring a stagnant religion up to date and, along the way, introduce new and deeper meanings to the old Judaic Scriptures. This is what made Jesus' message so compelling. It rang clearly as spiritual truth in the minds of the people.

Jesus mission was the same as that of all teachers of the Ancient Wisdom who are over- shadowed by the *Christos*--to purify old doctrines that had become stale and static or become, in the hands of the priesthood, the means to exert control over people. He wanted those who had the "ears to hear" to know that when a religion is institutionalized it loses its vital energy in a very short time. Soon, following the letter of the law becomes more important than understanding the philosophy behind it. This is precisely what Jesus was teaching to all who would listen– the real spiritual philosophy behind the letter of the law.

Pilate clearly did not like the way this new course of action was going. He cursed himself for having been drawn into this murderous web. His wife had made a special trip to him while he sat down on the judgment seat to tell of a dream she had that night. "Have nothing to do with this," she pleaded with him. "I have suffered pangs of guilt all morning because I have seen a vision of his innocence. No good can come of this!" Pilate, however, could only consider the political aspects of the event which now had a life of its own. He therefore had to somehow give the mob what it demanded and also make it look like it was their decision and not his.

His desperate thoughts brought him to his senses and he became focused on the task before him. Suddenly a plan entered his mind whereby he could get the Jews to accomplish their own ends. He knew the Chief Priests of the Sanhedrin had brought charges against Jesus out of spiritual envy. Their reason, always unspoken in public, was simply that Jesus could work miracles and raise the dead and the Chief Priests could not. If this continued, it would have the effect of deflating the influence of the Sanhedrin while raising that of Jesus. Pilate began to put his plan into action by first motioning for quiet. "Whom do you want me to release to you, Barabbas or Jesus, who is called the King of the Jews?" he said. "Which of the two do you want me to release for you?"

The crowd cried out, "Barabbas! Barabbas!"

Pilate again held up his hand for silence and then said, "Then what shall I do with the man you call the King of the Jews?"

"Crucify him!" they yelled

There is great spiritual significance in the rabble calling out for Jesus' crucifixion. This is an allegory for the destiny of any person of truth who tries to open up the eyes of the spiritually blind. It happens also every time some new idea is presented to the people. If they do not understand it, they "crucify" the person who brought it into being.

For example, Nikola Tesla brought the world the concept of alternating current—that which makes the world run today. But when he proposed a wireless energy system, J. P. Morgan crushed the whole thing because there was no way to charge for it. Thus Tesla was crucified by the capitalists.

The same thing has happened throughout history to almost everyone who has brought in new ideas and inventions. People will always crucify what they either don't understand or threatens the *status quo*.

Then Pilate again asked, "Why crucify him? I have found in him no crime deserving of death. I will therefore chastise him and release him, too."

The crowd shouted all the louder, "Crucify him, Crucify him!"

At this, Pilate set his plan in motion. Without a word he went over to a bowl of water that was near the judgment seat and, when he had the crowd's attention, he dramatically washed his hands, saying, "I am innocent of this man's blood. See to his death yourselves."

And a great many people present in the crowd answered, "His blood be on us and on our children!"

This last line and an earlier line spoken by Jesus: "It will be those who delivered me to you who will have the greater sin," (John 1:11) are so completely out of context with the Biblical narrative that they cry out for some kind of authentication. If ever there were grounds for evidence that Biblical Scriptures were deliberately altered so Jesus' crucifixion could be blamed on the Jews, these two lines provide them. Nevertheless, it is true that there was enough blame to go around for everyone involved.

Even so, there are still a lot of other scriptural inconsistencies in these trial scenes. When the Jewish elders brought Jesus to Pilate the first time, Pilate, not wanting to get involved with what he saw as a strictly religious dispute, said (John 18:31), "Take him yourselves and judge him by your own laws" and the Jewish scribes answered, "It is not lawful for us to put any man to death." Thus, if that is the law, it is wholly inconsistent with Pilate's declaring (Matt

27:24)--after washing his hands in a symbolic gesture to feign innocence--"I am innocent of this man's blood; see to it (his crucifixion) yourselves." Another bit of scripture (John 19:16) confirms this, declaring, "Then he [Pilate] handed him {Jesus] over to them [the Jews] to be crucified."

It is absolutely inconceivable that a strict Roman Governor such as Pilate would ever give up his prerogatives of punishment in such an incident. If it were not lawful for the Jews to put a man to death, then Pilate, especially in this high-profile case, would certainly not arbitrarily change the law, even to suit his own convenience. He would be reported to Rome immediately and his governing days–and career-- would be over. It follows then that Pilate was *the only person–the only authority--who could have actually pronounced a death sentence on Jesus!*

Furthermore, it was Roman soldiers who carried out the crucifixion. Why would these soldiers just forget their Roman allegiance and start taking orders from the Jews? Can we believe Pilate would turn his own soldiers over to the Jews to do *their* dirty work? The conclusion is obvious: Pilate, not the Jews, was *solely responsible* for Jesus' crucifixion.

Then Pilate, in his last act to pacify the crowd, released Barabbas to them and, turning to his own guard, he gave the order to have Jesus scourged, a flogging with a multi-tailed whip with pieces of bone and metal woven into the leather thongs. It invariably rips open a person's back and leaves it a bloody, pulpy mess.

After the scourging, the weary and weakened Jesus was taken back into the praetorium by the soldiers of

Pilate's guard. There, before the entire battalion, he was stripped and then clothed in a deep scarlet robe. Another soldier fashioned a crown of thorns that was pulled down on his head, drawing blood around his forehead. Then they put a reed in his right hand--which was to resemble a staff of office--and knelt down on their knees, bowing deeply and mocking him, shouting, "Hail, King of the Jews." When they were finished with their humiliation, they took back the garments and put Jesus' clothes back on him and led him outside for the death march to Golgotha.

When they reached the road, the commander of the guard seized a huge man called Simon of Cyrene and ordered him to carry the cross on which Jesus was to be crucified. And so the procession commenced with Simon in front followed by Jesus in custody of the Roman soldiers, followed by two other men who, due to their acts of thievery, were sentenced to be crucified on crosses set alongside Jesus.

In the Esoteric Doctrine of the Ancient Wisdom, each man has to allegorically carry his own cross to Calvary. This is a metaphor for one's following the Spiritual Path. Those who follow this path are, because of their beliefs, crucified (not literally, but in spirit) daily on the cross of Spirit and Matter, the vertical bar being Spirit and the horizontal bar representing Matter. This means that their concentration on things spiritual comes in conflict with those who are only concerned with things of a more materialistic nature. Thus the figure of the cross represents the matrix over which the raising of the "Christ Principle" takes place–from the depths of the

physical, below the horizontal bar of Matter, to the heights of Spirit, rising above the bar.

Jesus' teaching, in fact, was not Christianity as we know it today, but a very simple method of how to raise one's inner "Christ Principle" to unite with the Source of Spirit which is "God Consciousness." His method was truly the "Way, the Truth and the Life" of the Spiritual Path.

Jesus' method did not entail going to temple and listening to the exhortations of the priests to their congregations on how to be a good person. Jesus' way was more direct. It entailed just two modalities:

1) Meditation and studying the Esoteric Doctrine of the Ancient Wisdom

2) Service to one's fellow human beings.

In this manner the candidate for the Spiritual Path to Initiation served the dual aspects of life: Spirit and Matter. As the candidate disciplined himself to perform these two functions in his daily life, he eventually came into contact with the Ray of the Christ Principle which would then become his constant guide, raising him ever higher on the spiritual path.

This is true Christianity. This is what Jesus was teaching his disciples. He taught that these modalities exerted a direct positive influence on one's Karma which would bring a positive benefit not only in this life, but also in one's next incarnation. Thus one would continue striving toward God Consciousness lifetime after lifetime—continually raising one's

"Christ Principle" upward until the goal of complete unification with the Source, or God, was reached.

The most outstanding aspect of Jesus' teaching was that it did not entail or involve a priesthood! He was teaching his disciples the path of direct action in finding God while the rabbis and priests (and later, the ministers) were busy trying to exhort people to find God through their preaching. This was the source of their power and control in the community.

So the priesthoods wanted to be known as the holy keepers of the Keys to the Kingdom while Jesus was teaching his disciples how to reach that kingdom by themselves. Thus, as people listened to Jesus talk and nodded agreement with his methods, the Chief Priests saw their spiritual hold on the people slowly withering away. Thus they plotted his death.

As the processional continued on its way up the hill, a great multitude of people, including many women, joined them. The women were weeping and bemoaning Jesus' fate. Jesus told them, "Daughters of Jerusalem, do not weep for me, but weep for yourselves and for your children. For behold, the days are coming when they will say, 'Blessed are the barren, and the wombs that never bore, and the breasts that never suckled a newborn babe!' For they will begin to say to the mountains, 'Fall on us;' and to the hills, "Cover us' For if they do this when the wood is green, what will happen when it is dry?"

Most of the women were puzzled at Jesus' pronouncements, but his mother, Mary, being a disciple and therefore steeped in Jesus' Esoteric

Doctrine, probably knew her son was talking about the earth's evolutionary change that was to come some 2,000 or so years later when the Kali-Yuga, the "Age of darkness" would finally give way to the Satya-Yuga, the "Golden Age"–the "Age of Light." The Kali-Yuga ended in 1942 but cosmic change is never precipitate so the two ages tend to overlap. When these calamitous changes will happen, no one knows and anyone who says they can predict such things is wrong. As Jesus told his disciples, "No one knows except my Father in Heaven."

This change is said to be signaled by violent earthquakes and volcanic eruptions in the beginning ("when the wood is green") and later conclude ("when the wood is dry") with cataclysmic changes in the earth's surface, i.e., a polar shift causing the tectonic plates which comprise the surface of the earth to pull apart, drift around and join with others to create altogether new continents.

As one can see from the formations of the landmasses today, particularly how complimentary are the coastlines of Africa and South America, this same thing has definitely happened before.

Arriving at Golgotha, which means "the place of a skull," the soldiers stripped Jesus of his garments and since Jesus' tunic was woven from top to bottom without a seam, i.e., it was a valuable one-piece garment--they decided to cast lots for it instead of tearing it into pieces.

The Esoteric Doctrine tells us that a garment without a seam is the proper vesture of the *"mythical*

Christ." This is derived from the swaddling of the Egyptian dead in seamless material in order for them to become in the afterlife that what such an image symbolized--a *Karest* (or Christ). Thus the mummy was wrapped with a seamless bolt of material in hopes that by imitating the garment of the unseen Christ—which they knew was a high Spiritual Principle, not of the material world—one would actually become a Christ in the world of Spirit. The idea that Jesus had on a seamless garment is in agreement with this well-known (at that time) Egyptian myth. It was a symbol of honor.

Then they began to set up huge crosses on which Jesus and the two thieves were to be crucified. At the top of Jesus' cross there was nailed a sign that read "Jesus of Nazareth, the King of the Jews." It was written in Hebrew, Latin and Greek. Earlier, the Chief Priests of the Jews tried to convince Pilate to change it, arguing, "Since the place where Jesus is to be crucified is near the city and many Jews will therefore be able to read this title, so do not write 'The King of the Jews,' but '*This man said*, I am King of the Jews.'" Pilate looked at them sternly and shook his head. "What I have written, I have written," he said, dismissing them.

By keeping the declaration sparse, Pilate sent a succinct political message to all Judaism. He was saying, "Here is your Messiah, your King, and he is a dead man." In fact, Pilate's stinging message operates on a threefold level. Pilate was letting the Jews know in no uncertain terms that: 1) There is no such thing as a Messiah because a real Messiah

would be able to save himself, 2) If this, in fact, was really your Messiah, he is your Messiah no longer and, 3) This is what will happen to anyone who in the future might want to proclaim himself the King (Messiah) of the Jews.

This is strong imagery indeed! Pilate meant to convey nothing less because he wanted to project a strong, uncompromising image as a ruling governor. Although he certainly had enough troops to put down the occasional insurrection or slave revolt, he was virtually helpless against a truly massive uprising. An actual Messiah, which all Judaism held in their heart of hearts as the one who would release them from Roman bondage, was the only leader, real or imagined, who could ever organize a force strong enough to successfully challenge Roman control of the province. Thus, through vivid imagery, Pilate foreclosed on any future claims to Messiahship.

The symbolism of the Christ crucified between two thieves is an allegory of the Ancient Wisdom. Jesus represents the *Chrestos*–the neophyte on the path to full God Consciousness--the two thieves personify two powerful opposites. One is symbolic of the lower, mundane attractions of material life while the other represents the higher, spiritual realm of the Christ. They are portrayed as "thieves" in the symbolism of this tableau because each desires to "rob" the neophyte of his desire for the other.

* * *

WAS JESUS THE MESSIAH?

...Or the "Son of Man" or the "King of the Jews?"

The four gospels of the Bible—particularly the Gospel of Matthew—are brimming with evidence that Jesus was definitely not *the* Messiah. In comparing just a few key bible verses we find evidence of re-writing, and the elimination of text—all done to make it appear that Jesus was the Messiah.

Why? What would be the advantage to the Church of altering bible verses to make Jesus appear to be the real Emissary of God? Primarily, it would give Jesus a strong biblical lineage as a "Son of God," making it easier to establish belief in him as a consubstantial Deity who walked on the face of earth.

Similarly, by claiming Jesus as the Christ, Messiah, the Son of God *and* the Son of Man, it would give the Church a kind of moral advantage over the Jews who rejected Jesus and wanted him crucified. We can be sure that the Church had a vested interest in claiming Jesus as a "Christ" for Christians *and* as the rejected "Messiah" of the Jews—to the glorification of the former and the denigration of the latter.

We have already seen how this has played out in history. Ever since the first Nicene Council in 325 C. E., the Church has claimed Jesus unique among prophets, a "Son of God" who walked the earth literally as a God Incarnate. Thus Jesus became an eclectic God who was proprietary to the Catholic Church and this enabled the Church to position itself to all prospective worshipers and the world at large as the "one true church." This gave them a distinct advantage over other religions, but it was all a fabrication.

There can be little doubt that during the trial of Jesus before Caiaphas, Pilate and Herod Antipas, the charges against him had nothing to do with his being a Christ and everything to do with his being a potential Messiah.

Dr. Hugh J. Schonfield, author of the misguided but intriguing and well-researched book *The Passover Plot* (Random House, 1965) writes, "...the Jews of the time of Jesus were expecting a Warrior Messiah, one who would win military victories over the enemies of Israel, and in this way accomplish the deliverance."

It was this kind of Messiah who was expected to lead Israel out of bondage (i.e., Roman occupation) so it is easy to see why the eventual charge against Jesus was for sedition, i.e. the incitement of a rebellion against Rome. This is the only charge that got Pilate's complete attention and is precisely what led to Jesus' crucifixion, which was the Roman punishment for sedition.

Held up to the crowd as the "King of the Jews" the charge of sedition stuck where other charges didn't. This is very important to understand because he could not have been charged with sedition and crucified for either being or claiming to be a Christ.

With this in mind we can now see where the biblical account of the trial was re-written so as to sneak into the gospel narrative here and there the idea that Jesus was considered to be both the Christ and the Messiah. This certainly was a clever ruse and obviously designed to give Jesus a high spiritual status, but the fact is he was actually crucified as a Messiah, not a Christ.

Was he both a Messiah and Christ? This opens up a real convoluted can of worms. It is true that the concept of the Greek "Christos" can be translated as either the "Christ" or "Messiah" and both are *to a certain degree interchangeable* as both are an anointing. This is not an earthly anointing, one of oil, but is the conferring of a Spiritual Principle—The Christ Principle. This bestows a higher state of consciousness on the person so anointed and in that respect it could be said that Jesus was also a Messiah. However, he was not *the* Messiah.

What is a Christ or Messiah? Each is said to be a "Son of God" because they are "Messengers" sent to clarify and/or purify an ancient teaching that has gone stale and become weighted down with too many rules and regulations. But a Son of God is *not* to be confused with—and cannot be—a God Incarnate, because he is a human being born of woman. Thus the message of a Son of God is limited to certain nations and peoples in many different places on earth, *viz.* Buddha, Moses, Jesus, Confucius, Muhammad, Ramakrishna, Zoroaster, et al, are all Sons of God.

There is, however, *another Messiah* that is mentioned in the New Testament, but you would never know it unless you were familiar with ancient kabalistic concepts. This Messiah is not born of woman and thus exists on a Higher Plane of being than the Messiah or Christ who are Sons of God. In ancient Hebrew kabalistic scriptures this Messiah is known as the "King Messiah," but is not mentioned as such in Bible scriptures.

The "King Messiah," not being born of flesh, is, in fact, a High Essence or Force, a Cosmic Messenger, i.e., a direct Emissary of God who will bring a new teaching to the *whole planet* therefore he is referred to as a World Teacher. Since the King Messiah is a Judaic concept, that is how the idea of the "King of the Jews" came into being. But as happens in all religions, vital concepts become corrupted beyond all reason over time

. So, to sum up before we go on: Jesus is the Christ and also a Messiah and a Son of God. But the Messiah the Bible speaks of as coming in the "End Times" is actually the King Messiah who is also known as the Son of Man. Thus Jesus is not the Son of Man and he is definitely not the King Messiah.

Another clue to this conclusion is found in the scope of their teaching. As the founder of Theosophy, Mme. H. P. Blavatsky, wrote, "[Jesus' teachings] were never intended for the masses, for Jesus forbade the twelve to go to the Gentiles and the Samaritans (Matt. 10:5) and repeated to his disciples that the "mysteries of Heaven" were for them alone, not for the multitudes (Mark 4:2)." Thus we have only to look at the scope of Jesus' mission to see that it was limited to parts of Judea, whereas the work of a King Messiah is truly universal in nature. Thus Jesus could not have been the King Messiah and so is not the Son of Man.

Who *is* the actual Son of Man? To understand this concept we have to begin with a teaching of the Ancient Wisdom about the nature of the coming World Teacher. This completely new World Teacher is described in Sanskrit scriptures of Tibetan Buddhism as the "Lord Maitreya." His coming has been prophesied in Buddhist texts for over 8,000 years. He is also known in Buddhist teachings as the "Kalki Avatar" or "The White Horse Avatar" and his role is to bring a new spiritual teaching to earth.

This World Teacher is unique because he will be the first from another solar system. He is from the Dog Star, Sirius, and has been on this planet since the 50's. It is said he will make his appearance near the "End Times." His teaching will set the keynote of our spiritual future.

There is much to know about the Lord Maitreya, but this chapter is not the place for a full exposition of his nature. Suffice to say that **the Maitreya is actually the long-awaited *King Messiah*.** According to Mme. H. P. Blavatsky, the Kabala defines the King Messiah as "the Interpreter" of Divine Wisdom, Sophia, the Feminine Principle, and this is why the New Age is defined as the "Age of Women." Thus the Maitreya/Messiah will be a direct Emissary of God, so to speak, and his message for the world will be one of the need for more compassion.

For Christians, he will be the second coming of Christ. For Jews, he will be the appearance of Moses. For Buddhists, he will be the second coming of Buddha. For Muslims, he will be the second coming of Allah. Thus he truly will be a great Messianic Presence of the Highest Order—a true Son of Man.

Can this be proven? How can we really know that the coming Maitreya is both the Son of Man and the King Messiah and not Jesus? For this we need to look at the chapters (Matt. 22-26) in the New Testament that speak of the "End Times" or the "End Days"—those in which Jesus describes to this disciples the coming "wars and rumours of wars," the "sorrows," the future "coming of the Son of Man" and the "tribulation of those days." These happenings are said to signal the actual "end of the word" and provide the wherewithal for the second coming of Jesus who is said to refer to himself as the Son of Man in those times.

In Matthew 23 we find Jesus telling his disciples about what the terrible fate of the Scribes and Pharisees ("Ye hypocrites!"), would be in the future, concluding with (Matt. 23:36) "All these things shall come upon this generation."

The fact is: all the things he said *didn't* come on that generation—*unless* he was talking about what would happen to them in a future life when the Law of Karma would take its toll on them for their past misdeeds. We can be sure a man such as Jesus wasn't just blowing off steam, but talking about some other period of time. The only other future time period that he could possibly have meant is the "End Times" period.

Coincidentally, the first remark about the "End of Days" or the "End Times" comes in the third verse of the very next Chapter, Matt. 24:, and we find that the period in which all these bad things are supposed to happen has magically shifted from a "generation" to "the end of the world."

Jesus gave us an out, saying "of that day and hour knoweth no man, not the angels of heaven, but my Father only." (Matt: 24:36) but the question which begs explanation here is why Jesus would be telling his disciples about occurrences which, we know now, are thousands of years in the future? None of this makes any sense—*unless* he was talking about what is predicted to occur at the advent of the Lord Maitreya, i.e., the King Messiah and the new World Teacher.

Is that what he was talking about?

If we go to the Concordant Greek text and check out Matthew 24:3 we will find the King James version reads "end of the world," but in the original Greek text it reads "end of an eon." Is the end of an Eon the same as the end of the world? No! An Eon can best be described as an Age, so what we have here is the end of an Age, not the end of the world! This is not just a translation error because the difference is astounding. An error such as this has all the earmarks of being pre-planned!

An earlier book by Dr, Hugh J. Schoenfield, *The Authentic New Testament* (New American Library, 1958) translates that sentence as "the Consummation of an Age" and this is what modern Bible scholars consider an acceptable interpretation.

Is there a reference to some "Age" somewhere that is more specific; that shows us that Jesus at least knew what he was talking about?

In the ancient Hindu scriptures called "The Puranas" (translation: "of ancient times"), the various stages of the earth's evolution are delineated. According to the Puranas, there are four major Ages that keep repeating themselves throughout humanity's spiritual evolvement on the planet Earth. They are called "Yugas." The first is the Satya-yuga, the second is the Treta-Yuga, the third is the Dwapara-yuga and the last is the Kali-yuga.

When Jesus walked the earth, he and his disciples were immersed in the Kali-Yuga—also known as the "Dark Age" or the "Age of Iron." Thus when he made the comment about "the end of an Age," he had to mean the end of Kali-Yuga, the "Dark Age."

As was mentioned in the preceding chapter, we are in the time when the Kali-Yuga and the Satya-Yuga are overlapping each other. This places us in the beginning stages of the biblical Armageddon, an Age the ancient texts say will bring great cataclysmic changes to the face of the earth via a polar shift. Those same texts testify that this was how the ancient continent of Atlantis sank beneath the sea.

This is also the time that the ancient scriptures say the Lord Maitreya (the Son of Man) will come to earth. Thus, this has to be the very "Consummation of an Age" Jesus was talking about. His disciples, upon hearing his rant about the Scribes and Pharisees probably asked him when that would happen and Jesus told them: at the end of the Age when the Son of Man (the Maitreya) arrives. This is the only conclusion that makes sense! The idea that Jesus would switch to the third person and begin referring to himself as the Son of Man is not plausible.

Thus, by correcting all the errors in the Bible, we find the true facts to be: Jesus never claimed he was the Messiah. The Maitreya, not Jesus is the "Son of Man *and* the King Messiah." The "End Times" that Jesus was talking about to his disciples are to take place after the end of the Age of Kali-Yuga and before the full force of the Age of Satya-Yuga hits the earth.

And where are we today? We, the earth and the rest of its humanity are in the overlapping stages of the transition between the two Yugas. Are the "End Times" near? According to all the indications, they are. When will they occur" Fortunately, that is still the province of "Our Father in Heaven" and, just as Jesus said, "no one knoweth the day or the hour."

* * *

THE CRUCIFIXION

It's not what you think

Back at the crucifixion site, the soldiers continued their mocking of Jesus, offering him vinegar to drink and saying, "If you are the King of the Jews, let's see you save yourself!" and "He trusts in God, so let God deliver him from this crucifixion now!" Jesus was silent through all of this, but the two thieves also joined in mocking him from time to time. Jesus never said a word or showed any fear as the crosses were being prepared.

In those days, the Roman method of crucifixion included the act of impalement. Research done by French author Renée Dunan for his book on Julius Caesar (Re-titled for American consumption *"The Love Life of Julius Caesar,"* (E. P. Dutton & Company, 1931) has shown that there are four known surviving phrases dealing with the crucifixion. Justinius describes it as *"In crucem suffigere,"* or "to fasten to the cross." Seneca uses the phrase *"In crucem sedere,"* or "to sit on the cross." These two phrases indicate that the cross was nothing more than the pale.

Tacitus says *"cruci figere,"* or "to attach to the cross," and Petronius writes *"pendere in cruce,"* which means "to suspend on the cross." Also, the Greek texts always translate *"crux"* as *"skolops"* and *"stauros,"* the technical names for impalement.

In fact, in the New Testament, Matthew 27:31, the words "...and led him away to crucify him" are translated by the *Concordant Greek Text* as "led him into the impale." This is conclusive evidence that Jesus was actually impaled on the cross.

Martin Hengel's seminal book *Crucifixion* (Fortress Press, 1977) provides us with a well-researched view of the subject of crucifixion, probing its history and application from its use in ancient Persia to its function as punishment in Greek and Roman times as well as its use among the Jews. He writes "crucifixion and impalement...are closely related" and that its torturous nature was clearly meant to be a "visual deterrent." But the two have never been put together coherently until now.

We are not usually disposed to think of Jesus being impaled, but only the process of impalement answers the nagging question of why a person's body which was nailed to the cross with only spikes going through the palms of the hands and feet did not simply tear loose and slide down to the ground.

The process of crucifixion probably began with the cross lying flat on the ground. Jesus' hands were then nailed to the horizontal beam and each wrist was secured to the timber with ropes. Then, leaving a little slack in the body, they nailed his ankles onto the sides of the vertical beam. Next, they stood the cross upright, letting the bottom of the vertical beam slide into a deep hole which would keep it securely in place after dirt was packed in around it.

Two men with ladders (or some kind of scaffold which was built for this purpose) then scrambled up each side and hammered a 1½ to 2-foot long, slightly upward-curving spike from the back of the vertical beam through to the front at the approximate level of Jesus' buttocks. They then introduced the tip of the spike into Jesus' anus and continued hammering it, pushing it in far enough to where it passed under his pelvic bone so it would support the body on the cross. The two thieves got the same treatment.

The Roman spectacle of crucifixion by impalement was meant to be as savagely and tortuously cruel as possible because it had to accomplish two things: 1) to act as a visual deterrent to crime, and 2) to provide a theater of gore to satisfy the blood lust of those who came to watch.

The spike was the centerpiece of this typically gruesome Roman conception. When the cross was upright, it kept the victim's body from being torn loose by his own weight and sliding off. That was its practical use. But there was also a kind of diabolical sideshow, something to further attract viewer interest to the crucifixion proceedings.

With the spike thrust under the pelvic bone, but not yet coming through the body, a man could use the leverage of his arms and his legs to project his body outward, curving it away from the cross and thus preventing the spike from penetrating any further up and into his bowels.

But as one's arm strength gave out, one's body would slowly sink down on the spike, causing the spike to penetrate further along through one's maze of intestines.

Eventually, after leg strength also gave out, all leverage was lost and the body, of its own weight, would slump back against the vertical beam, driving the spike slightly upwards through the body's maze of vital organs until it pierced the stomach lining from the inside out, spewing blood and guts all over

the ground. Mercifully, death usually followed in a short time thereafter.

When it came to devising fiendish methods of torture and death, the Romans were without equal and left no bloodthirsty detail behind. Hardy onlookers would show up at every crucifixion to watch the proceedings and even bring food with them so they would be sure not to miss the gory climax. The more beastly onlookers would make bets on how long a person would last before his body gave out, or on which one might bring on a quicker death by forcing his body to descend on the spike–a kind of reverse *hara-kiri*.

On average, the spectacle could last up to two days depending upon a person's strength of resistance and his will to extend life as long as possible. This is what drew the crowds.

When Jesus' suffering on the cross was just beginning, the guards offered him a goblet of wine mixed with gall or myrrh. This was a kind of sedative, designed to relieve some of the pain. But when Jesus tasted what it was, he rejected the offer, choosing instead to experience his approaching death in full consciousness.

When the cross with Jesus attached to it was in place and he was already struggling with the movement of the spike, he looked with sorrow upon the Roman guards and then glanced skyward and said, "Father, forgive them for they know not what they do." In the back of the crowd, looking on from afar, were many women who had followed him from Galilee. Near to the cross was Jesus' mother Mary, his sister Mary (the wife of

Cleophas), Mary Magdalene and the only male disciple there, the beloved John.

When Jesus was able to focus on the nearer group he said to his mother, "Woman, from now on John will be your son." Then he gazed at John and said, "From this day forward she will be your mother." With this personal business taken care of, Jesus sighed and asked for water. To mock him, one of the soldiers gave him a sponge filled with vinegar. The Chief Priests, trying to arouse the crowd, yelled out, "He saved others but he cannot even save himself. He says he is the king of Israel. Well, if he is, let him come down now from the cross and we will believe him so."

The scribes bellowed, "He said he was a son of God and that he trusts in God, so lets see if God will save him now." Of course, this was all a form of pre-planned street theater meant to influence the people present and put Jesus on the same level as the Messiah, the King of the Jews.

One of the two thieves crucified with him also began to mock him saying, "If you are the Christ, save yourself and us." But the other thief cut him off, saying, "All of us must fear God in this case because we are all condemned to the same fate. However you and I are receiving our just due according to our deeds, but this man has done nothing wrong. Jesus, remember me when you come into your kingdom," he said.

Jesus looked directly at the condemned thief and said, "I promise you that today you will be with me in paradise."

Now it was the 6th hour (12 noon) and a strange darkness began to permeate the area. It would hang there for three hours. During this time the spike would complete its barbarous work. At the 9th hour (3:00 PM) Jesus cried out "My God, my God, how Thou dost glorify me!"

This phrase is usually translated in the New Testament as "My God, my God, why hast thou forsaken me," and quite a bit of theological thinking has gone into justifying it. However, the great theologian Mme. Helena P. Blavatsky showed conclusively that there was a mistranslation between the Greek and the Hebrew and two Hebrew glyphs were wrongly copied which resulted in the translation error. Since the Ancient Wisdom has always said that Jesus attained his Supreme Initiation on the cross, we can be confident that he was "glorified" rather than "forsaken" by his "Father in Heaven."

Now, knowing that death was near, Jesus said, "I thirst." One of the guards dipped a sponge into a bowl of vinegar and put it at the end of a long reed and lifted it up to Jesus' mouth. Jesus looked at the vinegar-soaked sponge and, recognizing that there was nothing left for him on earth, he probably bore his body down on the spike, causing it to pierce the outer flesh of his stomach, pouring his intestines onto the ground. Looking skyward he said, "It is finished. Father, into thy hands I commit my spirit!" With that, Jesus breathed his last and his head slumped over on his chest. He was dead.

At this moment, as it is stated in Matthew 27:51-53, "...the curtain of the temple was torn in two, from top to bottom; and the earth shook, and the rocks were split; the tombs also were opened, and many bodies of the saints who had fallen asleep were raised, and coming out of the tombs after his resurrection they went into the holy city and appeared to many."

In the above verses, the "curtain of the temple" is that ethereal "veil" which separates the physical world from the subtle, invisible worlds. That it was torn from "top to bottom" means that all of the invisible planes of existence became suddenly visible.

How did this happen? Jesus, embodied a powerful Spirit. Spirit is Energy—Psychic Energy. On his level it was like being connected to row of 10,000 dynamos. This mighty energy was emanated from Jesus not only to people, but to the land they walked on. In short, he kept everything around him—for 50 miles or more—in equilibrium.

When he expired on the cross, this energy was withdrawn at such a rate that it caused the earth around him to shake and split open. The energy released by this small earthquake was such that it raised the vibratory energy of everyone around and, for the moment, they became clairvoyant.

With such a broad tear in the earth, those peering on such a scene for the first time with physical eyes would see Celestial Beings as globes of light, much as the Angels are described. Thus they would be clearly seen as "saints" to people who only had that kind of reference for identification. Few were aware then of the existence of astral bodies and such.

The fact that it was reported "the tombs also were opened," demonstrates that the reporter did not have knowledge of the invisible worlds and described what he saw in his own terms. When one is allowed to "see into" the invisible astral worlds, one "sees" the dead—

actually those spirits still psychically attracted to earthly life. They are all around, walking about just as they did before they died. Therefore, unless one had esoteric spiritual knowledge and clairvoyance, one would immediately assume that somehow the tombs had to be opened in some way in order to let these people out. Even today the response to a similar occurrence would probably be the same.

With the darkening of the sky to almost blackness, the violence of a huge earthquake, the splitting up of huge boulders, the opening up of the invisible worlds to view and the sight of supposedly dead people walking around as if they were alive, it is no wonder that the Roman guards and other witnesses were shocked by what they saw. It is very understandable that they attributed it to the agony and death of a High Spirit and were ready to believe that Jesus truly must have been some kind of god-like person.

Evidently, the natural violence that followed Jesus' death didn't last long. It was just past the 9th hour (3:00 PM) on Friday when Jesus died on the cross and it wasn't until that evening that Joseph of Arimathea came to take the body down off the cross. Nevertheless, the Biblical narrative continues after Jesus' death with a passage which is extremely confounding.

In John 19:31-37, it is written: "Since it was the day of Preparation, in order to prevent the bodies from remaining on the cross on the Sabbath (for that Sabbath was a high day), the Jews asked Pilate that their legs might be broken, and that they might be taken away. So the soldiers came and broke the legs of the first and of the other who had been crucified with him; but when they came to Jesus and saw that he was already dead, they did not break his legs. But one of the soldiers pierced his side with a spear, and at once there came out blood and water. He who saw it has borne witness--his testimony is true, and he knows that he tells the truth--that you also may believe. For these things took place that the scripture might be fulfilled, "Not a bone of him shall be broken." And again another scripture says, "They shall look on him whom they have pierced."

This passage happens to be one of the most perplexing and conflicting group of verses in the entire New Testament. In the synoptic accounts of the gospels, it occurs *after* Jesus has expired on the cross, therefore the Jews who came to see Pilate about the bodies evidently assumed that Jesus and the two thieves would still be alive at that time. In asking to have their legs broken, the Jews wanted to be sure that the three would be dead in compliance with the sacred laws of the High Holy Days. Their mission was truly sacrosanct.

But we must ask the obvious question: Why break their legs before taking their bodies down from the crosses? Would the bodies have been taken down if they were still alive? No. So we must conclude that all three were *not expected to be dead.*

Thus the breaking of legs must have been a regular occurrence in order to complete the job of crucifixion. To break their legs would cause their bodies to settle quickly back down on the spike, causing it to pierce the stomach lining and inducing a quick death. Then their bodies could be disposed of according to law.

This is a dramatic validation that crucifixion did, in fact, include impalement. Because the soldiers found Jesus already dead, it is also reasonable that he hastened his own death by forcing his body down on the spike–an extremely heroic achievement. It indicates Jesus had no fear of death. And we can conclude that the two thieves used all their strength to cling to life as long as possible. The symbolic juxtaposition is dramatic, indeed.

Next comes a really bizarre portion of this same scripture: a soldier's piercing of Jesus side with a spear and a highly-emotional plea that what he did was really the truth. First we must ask why a soldier would pierce a dead man with his spear? Next we must ask why the writer of the passage would go to such inordinate lengths to swear that this illogical act was true, especially when his very choice of words actually indicates that he must expect his readers to find his explanation very hard to believe.

There are two rationales for the piercing and the verbose explanation of it and each leads to a similar conclusion: that this scripture was, in fact, altered to support a fictitious scenario. First, Shakespeare gave us an example of testimony that does not ring true when he wrote "Methinks thou doth protesteth too much!" Thus he showed us that a righteous man speaks truth simply, but a man seeking to hide the truth provides an over-abundance of supporting affirmations. In this case, this is the only passage of its kind in the entire Old and New Testaments. It reeks of revision and despite the grand exhortations of the writer for belief; the declamatory verbiage leaves a rhetorical trail that ends in disbelief.

Secondly, if the story about the soldier thrusting his spear into Jesus were left out of this particular scripture, it would be rock-solid proof that Jesus' crucifixion was indeed accomplished by impalement. Otherwise, where could the stomach wound have come from? This leads to the suggestion that this entire passage was deliberately re-written and added to in order to cover up the true nature of crucifixion, making it appear to be less severe than it really was. This would also explain the need to over-dramatize the truthfulness of such a revision because there were obviously people alive who undoubtedly knew all the savage details of crucifixion. They probably attended a crucifixion or else were regaled with gory stories of it by their family's elders.

Certainly all the people living throughout the Roman Empire at that time were aware of the method of Roman crucifixion just as the Jews were. The Romans, as occupiers of foreign lands, were not so kind as to have lesser, alternate forms of justice for different satellite countries. Their own sense of justice and order was based upon Roman Law which was designated to be the same everywhere for everyone and since crucifixion was supposed to be a deterrent to crime (particularly sedition, which Jesus was accused of) everyone must have been acutely aware of just what crucifixion entailed.

The big question remains: why would the church want to expunge the true nature of crucifixion from the scriptures? Was there a cover-up of the truth?

Certainly one reason was to deflect the curiosity of those Roman Pagans whom the church was trying to convert who might ask: "How can I be expected to follow a God who would allow his only begotten Son to experience such a horrible death?" Neither could these prospective converts help but wonder why Jesus, if he truly was, as the church claimed, a "living God," didn't save himself from death? They could easily point out that Old Testament Gods frequently brought plagues and catastrophes on those enemies hostile to them (on the Egyptian Pharaoh in Moses' case, for example), so why didn't God at least act to save Jesus–the Living God and His only-begotten Son–from his enemies?

To thoroughly understand why all this altering of scripture took place, even though it meant falsifying the Holy Bible, one has to become conversant with that thin sliver of time between 312 and 337 C.E. when Constantine I ruled the Roman Empire. This was a most unusual time because Constantine was not, at first, the sole governing emperor. He actually ruled the Western half of the empire while the Eastern half was ruled by his rival, Licinius. As any one would suspect, each had dreams of uniting the vast Roman Empire under a single emperor, themselves, therefore both rulers were plotting strategy to overthrow the other, merely waiting for the right opportunity.

In 313, Constantine and Licinius jointly signed the "Edict of Milan" which granted protection to the Roman Catholic Church and especially decreed that Catholicism could operate freely throughout the empire as a lawful religion. On the surface, this edict appeared to be a wholly religious decision, however Constantine, whose talents as a brilliant military strategist went far beyond the battlefield, envisioned using the Catholic Church as an outright arm of his military conquests. He saw--as all wise emperors with conquest in their blood have since seen--that religion could be used as a potent social force in unifying a country and even in occupying conquered territory. At that particular time, the Western half of the empire was 20% Christian while Licinius' Eastern half was 50% Christian and Constantine anticipated that a *Christian* legion marching into the Eastern provinces of the empire would be welcomed immediately by half the population as saviors rather than conquerors.

Thus Constantine began his complex plan. He first engaged the local Catholic bishops and priests in religious discussions during casual walks in his ornate palace gardens. Through these chats he not only gained insight into the finer points of Catholic Doctrine, but also found out that not all Catholic Churches in his realm were preaching from the same page; that many bishops, especially those in North Africa, were using a diverse assortment of gospels--many of them outright Gnostic--in their sermons to parishioners. Many bishops, including Arius of Alexandria, were teaching doctrines that were derived from the earlier Marcionites, who also preached Gnostic concepts. Thus there was not a single doctrine for all Catholic Churches. This was in direct conflict with Emperor Constantine's sense of uniformity and order and he told the bishops that his desire was to see the Catholic Church expand its authority throughout the realm, but that it was virtually impossible until the church's doctrines were truly catholic everywhere.

Constantine wanted a uniform religious front–a true Holy See with hierarchal channels of authority--with every church and every bishop on the same page and preaching from the same scriptures. With that accomplished, he could then orchestrate a campaign to convert the Roman citizens to what would now be a distinctly new Roman religion. Then, as the *de facto* head of the Catholic Church (Constantine was also the *Pontifex Maximus* of the Roman Empire, a holy deified "Minister of God") he was assured that the bishops would do what he wanted in return for the state-protected expansion of the Catholic religion. In this manner he would gain complete control over the entire Roman Empire not only militarily, through his chain-of-command as emperor, and socially, through the Roman Civil Service, but also by being the top man in the empire's religious chain-of-command.

Although a lifelong Pagan himself, Constantine undertook a series of projects planned to ingratiate himself further with the Catholic Fathers. First, he razed several Pagan temples and gave their lands and riches to the Church. Then he began placing Catholics, including bishops, in the mid-to-higher levels of the Roman civil infrastructure. This is how Christianity became the servant of the government throughout the empire, especially among the elite who were the scions of Roman law and fashion in the smaller cities, and constituted a new hierarchy of unified power that descended from God through to the Emperor to Roman civil authority and finally down to the Roman people. This exact scenario has been repeated over and over throughout history and is still in use today.

In his book *Authority and the Sacred* (Cambridge University Press, 1995), author Peter Brown writes, "...we should not underestimate the long-term impact of a new, more drastic definition of monotheism on notions of authority among lay elites. Christian exhortation presented the elites with a new model of power. It assumed a chain of command drawn as starkly on earth as it was in heaven. An emperor on active service for the Christian God was linked to his upper-class subjects and, through these, to all inhabitants of the empire. Power over others, superiorities of wealth and culture, were not to be taken for granted. They were direct gifts from a High God. Their principal justification on earth was their active employment in the service of His Church."

Thus the Catholic Church *knowingly* became the submissive servant to the wide-ranging political ambitions of the Emperor Constantine. And it is not unrealistic to say in all candor that from this point on any chance of the world ever becoming a truly democratic unity of cultural diversity was lost. Every attempt to do so, including the founding of America-- meant primarily to be a nation of religious diversity —has failed, victimized by religions who claim their authority comes from God.

After one failed try, Constantine finally defeated Licinius in a decisive battle in 324, C.E., and became the sole Roman Emperor. Soon he called for an Ecumenical Council of Catholic bishops to meet in Nicea in 325 C.E. 318 bishops came to what they considered was the most important conclave in the short life of the Church. It was Constantine himself who presided over the conclave, giving all present the distinct impression that he was the leader of this newly organized church. To be sure, almost everyone there knew that Constantine had co-opted the church leadership and that they were expected to do his bidding. But they were also imminently aware that despite the rules and laws they were to pass, the real prize was the opportunity to promulgate Catholicism throughout the Roman Empire under the emperor's protection—the first unification of church and state for the ever-ambitious Catholic Church.

The first major act of the Council of Nicea was to set forth a uniform doctrine that all the bishops in attendance could agree to. Thus the following creed became the revised root dogma of the Roman Catholic Church.

THE NICENE CREED

"We believe in one God the Father almighty, Maker of all things visible and invisible; and in one Lord Jesus Christ, the only begotten of the Father, that is, of the substance of the Father, God of God, light of light, true God of true God, begotten not made, of the same substance with the Father, through whom all things were made both in heaven and on earth; who for us men and our salvation descended, was incarnate, and was made man, suffered and rose again the third day, ascended into heaven and cometh to judge the living and the dead. And in the Holy Ghost. Those who say: There was a time when He was not, and He was not before He was begotten; and that He was made out of nothing; or who maintain that He is of another hypostasis or another substance, or that the Son of God is created, or mutable, or subject to change, the Catholic Church anathematizes.

This done, the Council of Nicea, after much debate, adopted these additional concepts as canon law:

1. The church was granted the power of anathema.

    --This gave the Church the power to silence any opposition.

2. Jesus was declared to be the consubstantial Son of God and because he was deemed "begotten" and not "made," he was proclaimed to be immaculately conceived.

    --This declaration was by a <u>vote</u> of the council with two bishops voting "no."

3. The council declared that Jesus "suffered" for "our Salvation" and was also "resurrected" and "ascended into heaven."

    --This is part of the cover-up, designed to provide a rationale for Jesus' Crucifixion.

4. It was proclaimed that Jesus would "judge the living and the dead" while in heaven.

    --With this, the church established the concept of "fear of judgment" in the minds of the masses. This was one of

> the keys to both religious and political control over the populace as non-believers would now run the risk of being declared heretics which meant their souls would burn in hell.

5. The "Holy Ghost" was declared to be the third person of the Trinity.

> --The concept of the Trinity is never mentioned in the New Testament and is in fact a female Pagan symbol which the church co-opted from the Gnostics.

5. It was affirmed that any one who did not believe in church doctrine would be declared anathema (cursed and excommunicated) by the church.

> --The implication was that the state would see to the punishment.

It should be pointed out that all of the above dogmatic rules and procedures which came out of the Council of Nicea in 325 C.E. were made up and issued by *men*, not God, even though the Church always says authority came from God.

One of the more important reasons the council was convened by Constantine was to deal with an Alexandrian bishop by the name of Arius (256-336, C.E.) who advocated a concept of the Christ as being not a person but a Spiritual Principle, an idea rapidly gaining adherents throughout the Alexandrian portion of the empire.

Arius' teaching took a decidedly different view of Jesus' life. He denied that Jesus was consubstantial (homoousia) with the Father and claimed that the "Christ" was of a different essence, a divine transcendental principle that was in existence before the world was even created.

Arias' view of The Christ was essentially that of the "Christos," the Christ as a *Principle* and not as a Christ-in-the-flesh, *viz*., Jesus. Reasoned in this more enlightened manner, Arias' theology is in line with that of the Ancient Wisdom. He saw Jesus as a human being who had spiritually ascended to the point where he was anointed by the Christ Principle. Arias also dismissed the idea of a Christ-in-the-flesh who was divine, thus, to him Jesus was certainly not divine because any human incarnation on the earthly plane cannot be, as Paul also stated, consubstantial with God.

Of course, Arias' teaching was a huge threat to Constantine's religious ideal of theological uni-uniformity. Constantine wanted a simple God that the illiterate masses could quickly relate to. He didn't want the Church to teach spiritual metaphysics to the masses, he wanted instant identification and history has proven that a graven idol always succeeds where others do not.

Like any enemy of the emperor, Arius had to be crushed. Thus, in return for Constantine's support, the good fathers carried out his unwritten mandate and, in a council session, declared Arius a heretic and his teaching as anathema to the Catholic Church. This is how the church would forever handle any questions of its supposed revealed divine authority.

Thus began what was to become a Catholic reign of terror as all Pagan and Gnostic books, rituals and sacred religious teachings and doctrines--anything which might detract from the newly-created dogma of what the church was now pushing as the world's "one true religion"--were quietly gathered up and secreted away to the Catholic Church's library or simply burned. Included were all the precious writings of the early Christian mystics they could find.

Joseph Campbell, in his book *The Power of Myth*, called this the "vandalism of an age." But it was much more than that. It changed the practice of religion from a thing of spiritual purity to one of mundane deceit, lies and misrepresentations which have been subsequently used as theological rationales for countless wars and murders in the name of what in reality is a false God.

After the Nicean Council, the Roman Catholic Church was free to create doctrine and dogma at will as long as it satisfied the political needs of its protector, Constantine. Thus the wholesale marketing of Christianity to the Pagans and gentiles began, the Jews being only marginal in the whole scheme of things.

Constantine observed that Pagans were already using the steps of Christian churches for their sun worship, so he knew that if he was to convert Pagans to Christians he would have to make Christian symbols of worship more Pagan-like in order to more easily facilitate acceptance. Thus, with the consent of a completely co-opted priesthood there began a wholesale alteration of Christian doctrine to make it more palatable to the Pagans worshipers.

Constantine, himself a Pagan, worshiped Mithras, the Persian Sun God, whose natal day was December 25th. On the reverse side of Constantine's coin-of-the-realm was inscribed "To the invisible Sun, my guardian." The Mithraic mysteries which he followed embraced baptism, a Eucharistic feast, confession, resurrection from the dead and a contingent of angels, complete with places called "Heaven" and "hell." Thus it was soon proclaimed that the birthday of Jesus would now be celebrated on December 25th This just happened to be the venerable Pagan "Day of the Sun" (Sun-day) and this became the day of worship of Jesus Christ.

Even Eusebius of Caesarea writes in his *Life of Constantine* that "in order to render Christianity more attractive to the Gentiles, the priests [of Christ] adopted the exterior vestments and ornaments used in the Pagan cult."

The church also adopted several old rituals including alter candles, incense and the ringing of bells and, as mentioned before, they stole the Holy Trinity from the Gnostics, eliminated the feminine principle from it and turned it into an all-male line of Apostolic Succession from God to Jesus to Peter to the pope (The "Vicar of Christ" on earth) and thence to the priesthood. All claimed the authority of God.

Thus the Church was able to claim a proprietary continuity of "revealed" doctrine from God down to the pope and the church priesthood.

The only problem was they had to fudge the bit about Peter founding the church. Their claim to this comes from Matthew 16:81 where Jesus is given to say, "I say to you that you are Peter, and upon this rock I will build my church."

This was accepted scripture since before the King James version of the Bible, but the problem is that the word "church" was not even in use during the time the scriptures were written! Thus we find again a convenient re-writing of scripture in order to support a fabricated doctrine.

And so, after all this detailed presentation, we finally come to our dénouement: the question: "Why?" Why did the church fathers alter the sacred scriptures of the New Testament to cover up the true nature of the act of crucifixion? What did they have to gain from this?

The answer lies in the realm of political necessity. With the creation of a brand new *Roman* religion and given the absolute necessity of doing *Roman* Emperor Constantine's bidding to convert the masses to this new, cobbled-together doctrine, it is entirely believable that the *Roman* Pagans and gentiles would never accept a *Roman* Catholic religion which had a prominent *Roman* Governor, Pontius Pilate, responsible for the crucifixion of what the *Roman* Catholic Church was now calling their proprietary "living Son of God on Earth."

Constantine was out to use this new religion to pacify and control his people, not incite them to rebellion. Thus the pressure was undoubtedly passed down to the Church fathers to come up with a more politically correct version of the trial of Jesus, one that neutralized the role of Pilate and, by necessity, scapegoated (who else?) the politically inconsequential Jews. With this done, only one other thing was missing: how to make Jesus' torturous crucifixion acceptable to a public which already knew what crucifixion was about.

This was no small problem and it was not one which could be solved by political pressure. For the church bishops, the issue now became how to give Jesus' death a religious meaning that would be bold enough to overcome the overwhelmingly distastefulness of the nature of crucifixion.

The solution the church fathers came up with (which, as we have seen, became doctrine at the Nicean Council) was both brilliant and audacious. They simply proclaimed to all that Jesus suffered crucifixion voluntarily to save all humanity from sin. This the church rolled out into history as the venerable "Christ died for our sins."

This made-up story, with absolutely no basis in fact, was to become the main slogan around which this new theology would be based. Would people believe it?

It really didn't matter, because in the Roman World the word of the Church was now backed by Roman Law and Roman Legions and above all the Church's authority to declare anything it didn't like anathema or heretical. As Mme. H. P. Blavatsky noted, "Christianity was promulgated at the point of a sword."

On one hand we have to appreciate the stark audacity of the church fathers when they finally realized the great opportunity given them when the Emperor Constantine chose them to spread the gospel of Catholic Doctrine to the ends of the Roman Empire—and do it under Constantine's protection! Thus they lost no time in producing a fictitious, patch-quilt doctrine that required them to use all the cleverness and cunning of a slick patent medicine salesman.

The thing is: they had nothing to fear. There were no amateur theologians in the Roman rabble so who was going to expose them? On the other hand they knew that in just three generations all memory of actual events would pass from the public mindset and a lie would become the truth. They knew that if they had the discipline to hold to their story everything they invented would become fact eventually. Their ultimate goal: to get people to believe that what we now call religion began with Jesus and has continued ever since under the authority of the Catholic Church.

Of course, the visible symbol of a deified Jesus soon became an effigy of him nailed to the cross. This constantly projected to all worshipers his suffering, reinforcing the idea that he endured crucifixion—gave up his life—to free humanity from sin. Every Catholic Church has a figure of Jesus hanging on a cross displayed prominently during every service. It is displayed prominently in every Catholic home. It is seen everywhere as a symbol of Catholicism. It has actually become one of the most dominating symbols in the world.

Now, try visualizing that symbol with a spike thrust though Jesus anus, extending out though his stomach. Do you get the picture?

This is why the Catholic Church needed a cover-up. They needed to put a cap on the cruel method of impalement. People would simply not believe that a Living God on earth would have to undergo such a heinous torture, especially since it was reserved for the worst seditionists.

Thus in order for their fiction to become truth over time–and the church certainly understood the need for patience over the long haul—they had to stop crucifixion from being used as a punishment and then destroy all records of the nature of the act.

That could only be done if crucifixion was banned in all the Roman provinces. Thus in 337, near the end of his life when the emperor was frail and in bad health and on his deathbed, the church fathers got him to sign an edict banning crucifixion. As a reward, he was finally baptized a Christian–when he was much too weak to resist.

Now, 1700+ years later, the crucifixion cover-up is still going strong, deceiving all who read the Bible. And what became of Constantine? Even though he was an avowed butcher, murdered his wife, cut up his nephew into pieces, murdered two of his brothers-in-law, killed his son, Crispus, and smothered to death a monk in a well, the Catholic Church, without apology, made him a Saint!

* * *

THE "RESURRECTION"

Did Jesus really arise from the dead?
The news that Jesus' body was gone from its sepulcher spread quickly. Two of the Roman guards who were at the sepulcher immediately went into town and told the chief priests of the Sanhedrin all that had happened. After conferring with each other for awhile, the priests gave each guard a large sum of money and told them to tell people that Jesus' disciples had come during the night and had stolen the body while the guards slept. Because sleeping on watch was punishable by death, the priests also told the guards they would handle any repercussions with their commander, the military governor. Thus the Sanhedrin, in a conspiracy with the Roman governor, put its own spin on Jesus' so-called resurrection.

The Christian Church would have us believe that Jesus was resurrected in his physical body, pointing out that his body was gone from the sepulcher and that he later appeared "in-the-flesh" to his disciples.

To say that the church has a lot riding on this scenario is an understatement, because it is the sole visible rationale for Jesus' divinity and, therefore, serves as the entire foundation upon which Christendom is built.

On the other hand, if there were other ways Jesus could appear to his disciples, i.e., other than in a physical body, the whole rationale for the Christian Religion might just be in jeopardy.

The doctrinal foundation of the church would become even more unbelievable if Jesus' appearance to his disciples was also seen as a message of actual proof that an after-death state of being was possible for them too, in fact possible for anyone. What then?

Early Sunday morning, Mary Magdalene, the "other Mary," Peter and John went to the sepulcher and saw that the stone that blocked its entrance (or exit) had been rolled away. The guards said an earthquake did it. The two Marys said it was the work of an angel. They said that an angel of the Lord descended from heaven and rolled back the stone from the door of the sepulcher and sat on it. The angel's countenance, they said, was like lightning and his raiment white as snow and for fear of him the keepers quivered in their shoes and appeared to be frozen in their tracks.

The guard's report that there was an earthquake is probably a rationale for the rolling away of the stone from the sepulcher by the angel. All angels have the ability to use their Psychic Energy for such occasions. This is the same kind of high energy that infused Jesus' body. According to the Ancient Wisdom, this is a God-like power when highly developed and can only be used in special circumstances by an advanced being who has mastered its principles.

It is the same energy that lifted and moved the blocks of the Great Pyramid of Cheops (The idea that the pyramids were built by slave labor is, and

always has been, preposterous). Without such esoteric knowledge, the guards very likely imagined or invented the idea of an earthquake in order to rationalize in their own minds--considering their vastly limited knowledge--the moving of the stone.

John, the beloved disciple, raced to the opening of the sepulcher and looked inside. He saw the linen burial clothes arranged neatly on the floor, but did not go inside. The more rambunctious Peter went right in and saw the linens and the napkin headwrap. He must have said something about Jesus having risen, because John now went inside to see for himself.

The disciples went away, but Mary Magdalene remained. Suddenly, two angels appeared and said to her, "Woman, why do you weep? Mary Magdalene answered, "Because they have taken my Lord away and I don't know where they have taken him." After saying this, she turned around and her peripheral vision saw a man standing nearby. It was Jesus, but she didn't recognize him immediately. Then Jesus, as the angel had, asked her, "Why are you weeping? Whom are you looking for?"

Mary Magdalene looked stunned and at first thought the man was the gardener and said to him, "Sir, if you have taken him away, please tell me where I can find him and I will be responsible for his body." Jesus looked straight at her and gently said, "Mary." Mary was startled, but she knew the voice. Turning, she saw Jesus and, bowing her head, she uttered, "Master."

Much has been made over the fact that it was a woman who first had the privilege of seeing Jesus in his after-death state and proclaiming such to the other disciples. This is very meaningful because all of the known disciples were men. Was Mary Magdalene also a disciple? Undoubtedly, she must have been. What is most significant, however, is that all Jesus' male disciples betrayed him, leaving him when he was arrested. The very fact that Mary Magdalene was not subjected to that test is esoteric proof that her love for Jesus was not only pure and steadfast, but the kind of unyielding love a disciple is supposed to have for his/her guru.

Mary Magdalene quickly moved to embrace Jesus, but he suddenly stepped back a bit and said, "Please don't touch me for I am not yet ascended to my Father, but go to my brethren and tell them I am ascending to my Father, and your Father, and to my God and your God."

Why didn't Jesus want Mary Magdalene to touch him? Why didn't Mary Magdalene recognize Jesus at first? These two legitimate questions, prompted by the narration itself, are undeniable proof that Jesus appeared to Mary Magdalene, and later to his other disciples, in *other* than a physical body. It is evident that Jesus' after-death body was therefore more similar to that of the angel who spoke to Mary Magdalene–the one whose radiance appeared as lightning–than it was to a physical body.

The vibrations of such as the angel's body are so high–projecting great Fiery Energy--that anyone who would have touched it would have brought great harm to themselves. It would be very similar to touching lightning. This would not have been the case with a physical body.

In fact, to believe that Jesus was raised from the dead in his physical body is simply absurd! This idea got started because of the imaginary scene in the Bible of Jesus "raising Lazarus from the dead" – a scurrilous fiction.

Mme. H. P. Blavatsky tells us that "'Laz' (equal to Ras) means to be raised up, while 'aru' is the name of the mummy. With the Greek terminal 's' this becomes Lazarus." This name somehow found its way into the Bible as a fellow named "Lazarus" who was raised from the dead. This is, however, a story based on Egyptian initiatory rites in which the adept is "born again," i.e. "resurrected" from the "dead "– a mundane consciousness – to a "new consciousness," meaning a raised consciousness to the level of *Christos* or the Christ Principle.

Thus we have yet another example where the translators of the Bible changed this event in order to once more bring a sacred spiritual principle down to the level of the fleshy mundane world. Either that or they mis-translated it out of complete ignorance.

The actual story of Lazarus is something entirely different from what is related in the Bible. Thus, when Jesus arrived at Lazarus, tomb, he had been buried there already for four days. Jesus was asked by Lazarus' sister if Lazarus would arise and Jesus assured her he would, "arise" being a metaphor for ascension to Heaven. However, his sister thought he meant he would arise on Judgment Day. Jesus then says, according to the Bible, "I am the resurrection, and the life: he that believeth in me, though he were dead, yet shall he live: And whosoever liveth and believeth in me shall never die."

Thus those church fathers who re-constructed this scene took the opportunity here to slip in a passage fusing the man Jesus to the Principle of the Christ. A more accurate translation would be: "The Christ Principle is the resurrection, and the life: he that believeth in the Christ Principle, though his body is matter and dies, yet shall his consciousness live: And whosoever lives by the Christ Principle and believes in it, his consciousness shall live on eternally." It was through such falsehoods that the early church sought to mislead people into the belief that Jesus was a God walking upon the earth.

The question of there being different types of bodies is answered in Paul's First Epistle to the Corinthians, he writes of resurrection in general: (Cor. I-15:35), "But some man will say, How are the dead raised up? and with what body do they come?"

This statement implies there is more than one after-death body. Later on, Paul elaborates: (Cor. I-15:40), "There are also celestial bodies and bodies terrestrial: but the glory of the celestial is one, and the glory of the terrestrial is another."

This confirms that there are two different kinds of bodies, but it leaves us wondering what the difference is between them. Are there other kinds we are not aware of?

The answer comes later on in Corinthians when Paul explains the two bodies, writing: (Cor. I-15: 42), "It (one's physical body) is sown in corruption (of the earth); it is raised (at death) in incorruption (in the invisible spiritual realm)." Paul concludes his lesson in after-life bodies 10 verses later, teaching: (Cor. I-15:52) "...for the dead shall be raised incorruptible, and we shall be changed." None other than Jesus says (Matt. 22:30) that people will be, after death, "like angels in heaven." So the only conclusion which can be reached is that Jesus' after-death body was at least angelic–a glorified celestial body with the radiance of lightning, or, more accurately, Fiery Cosmic Energy.

For the rest of us who are not on Jesus' spiritual level, the Esoteric Doctrine of the Ancient Wisdom says that the "corruptible body" mentioned by Paul is the physical (terrestrial) body that dies and is buried, cremated or interred and that the "incorruptible" body is the "astral double" or "doppelganger" that is known in spiritual metaphysics as the "astral body."

The astral body--and we all have one--is that sometimes visible, most times invisible, outline of the physical body which is frequently what people see when they say they have seen a ghost.

Although the astral body is usually invisible to the human eye, there are a number of recorded instances where friends and family have seen and talked to loved ones after they have died.

What they actually were seeing was the dead person's astral body (this would be, according to

Paul, the incorruptible body, i.e., it would not be of the physical realm) and the reason they saw it was due to a strong, loving, spiritual link to that person, with the accent on "loving."

A week after he was first seen, during Jesus' second visit to his disciples, he had by then "ascended to my Father"–which means that after a short transitional period (three days, just as he had predicted), he was able to place all these High Fiery Energies completely under his control. Thus he was able to–as all High Souls are–create for himself what in the Ancient Wisdom is known as a "densified astral body." This is a type of body all Mahatmas (High, Transcended Souls) use when it is necessary to materialize in a body on the earthly plane of existence. It takes whatever form a Mahatma chooses it to be and appears to the earthly eye exactly as any other physical body. It is built by thought energy.

The key difference between an astral body and a densified astral body is that the density of the latter comes from atoms of earthly matter, so it appears to be a body more of the earth than of spirit. This is why Jesus was able to appear in the midst of his disciples while all the doors were closed. He could instantly "build" a densified astral body–a double of his earthly body–on the spot as an act of will and later disintegrate it the same way, disappearing from view.

Because the vibrations of the densified astral body were of the lower, earthly plane, it even allowed "doubting" Thomas to touch his wound without getting hurt.

Thus, to expand on Paul's teaching, we are all born in a "corruptible" (physical) body and when we die we are "raised up" (ascend in spirit) in a spiritual (incorruptible) body–the astral body. But those who are *really* High Souls– Mahatmas, Jesus, etc.–will transcend into a "*glorified* astral (Fiery, celestial) body" after death. Esoterically, in Buddhism, this is known as the *Nirmánakâya* body as it is illuminated with the radiance of the energy from the highest plane of all being--Atma.

That is why such a High Soul must go through a transitional period in order become accustomed to the new, Higher Energies. It takes time to bring these vital energies under control and master them in order to create a densified astral body.

So the question remains, what happened to Jesus' physical body? Why was it missing from the sepulcher?

Mme. Blavatsky writes that ordinary human beings are "an aggregation of atoms temporarily united by a mysterious force called the life principle. The only difference between a living and dead body is that in one case that force is active and in the other it is latent. When it is entirely extinct, the many molecules obey a superior attraction which draws them asunder and scatters them through space."

The life principle Mme. Blavatsky is talking about is Psychic Energy. Psychic Energy, the "God Essence," is in every atom in the universe, including the atoms of our body. We drew these atoms to us when we were born. When we die, we lose our Psychic Energy and as our cells decay, the atoms disperse to whence they came. This separation allows us to free our so-called "Astral Body" from our atoms, thus disintegrating the physical body. This takes time unless the body is cremated. It is the Astral Body that is connected for a time to our consciousness from our past life and the two, enjoined, are what enter the Astral Plane for our sojourn there in the invisible worlds.

Jesus, however, was no ordinary person—not like us at all. Through countless lifetimes of raising his Christ Consciousness, his body chemistry became so refined that he radiated Light Energy, i.e., Psychic Energy. If one had the eyes to see it, they could see a distinct glow around him. This is his healing energy. This is why his mere touch or glance could heal or change a person's life.

His body was so highly charged that his spiritual vibrations would shine like the sun, but when he died on the cross, his energy force ceased and was drawn back into his body. Thus, after Jesus' body was put in the sepulcher, it disintegrated. This was not magic, but science.

Einstein's simple equation ($E=MC^2$, i.e., Energy (E) equals Matter (M) multiplied by the speed of light squared, shows us that *Matter and Energy are the same thing,* we find that the molecules of Jesus body were made up of atoms which were vibrating at an extremely high rate, if not the speed of light.

This means that on the sub-atomic level the positrons (anti-electrons) of the atoms annihilated the electrons. This produced an explosion of energy that disintegrated all of the atoms of Jesus body. And that is the operational word: disintegrated. In a split second they were all released from physical bondage.

So, with this esoteric knowledge we can finally deduct that Jesus' body was disintegrated and his Spirit was resurrected in a combined "glorified," "celestial" and incorruptible" body, just as St. Paul described in First Corinthians. And it wouldn't hurt to hear again the exclamation of St. Paul who in Corinthians I, 15:50 writes, "Now, I say this, brethren, that *flesh and blood cannot inherit the kingdom of God*."

What can be plainer? Think of it logically? How can a flesh and blood body exist in the invisible spheres of the after-life state of being? Does the Church think Paul was lying? And if Jesus did rise in a physical body, why isn't he still appearing, helping us out now when we need him most!"

The whole scenario of Jesus' crucifixion, the disintegration of his body and his appearances to his disciples in a densified astral body occurred because of his mission in this life. His actions demonstrated to his disciples principles that he had been teaching them for three years. Thus he was able to indelibly burn his teaching into the minds and souls of his disciples by *personal example* with visual proof of the truth of a continuing existence and an after-life. The lesson was: Don't be afraid of death. It is merely a change of energy and *your consciousness continues in the invisible planes after your earthly body dies*.

So now imagine that you are one of Jesus' disciples. For three years he has been teaching you the most sacred truths of the Esoteric Doctrine of the Ancient Wisdom. He has taught you the intricacies of Karma ("whatsoever a man soweth; that must he also reap") and the fact of

Reincarnation ("who didst sin, this man or his parents?") and all the ins and outs of life and death including transcending and continuing life after death in a densified astral body. If you were an attentive disciple, you discovered that a single theme connected each facet of the many truths he taught: That which is invisible and of Spirit is real and everlasting and that which is of matter is perishable and therefore an illusion. This entire teaching is contained in his single admonition (Matt. 6:20) to "Lay up for yourselves treasures in Heaven" (not on earth) and to "Seek ye first the Kingdom of Heaven."

   He taught you all the basic tenets of his doctrine, especially that the goal of following the spiritual path was to raise the vibrations of the Christ Principle within your own being until you, in a future lifetime, reached the Highest Point of Being. He told you that if you purified your thoughts and developed your heart energy and lived an honorable and ethical life and were of service to others and to the common good of all, you could, through your own efforts, eventually reach that point where you could also become a Master of Spirit–just as he had done. Finally, he taught that as a Master of Wisdom you would be able to bring all matter under your control!

   As a disciple, you believe Jesus and have faith in him, but still, all these things he's telling you are purely theoretical and until you have verifyable proof that they can actually be achieved, all these lessons must remain as much an abstract to you as Jesus' wound was to "Doubting Thomas"

Thus Jesus, as the Ancient Wisdom tells us all Great Teachers do, impressed his teaching of the Esoteric Doctrine of the Ancient Wisdom on his disciples in a way they would never forget—in the only way that would make spiritual sense—by actually sacrificing his life as proof of the veracity of his Teaching.

Just as Jesus previously taught his disciples: "Greater love hath no man than to lay down his life for his friends," now his disciples had their proof. It was indelible proof that would stay with them forever.

* * *

EPILOGUE

What was covered up?

The fact is: the cover-up of the method of crucifixion by the Catholic Church leads to a hornet's nest of more cover-ups sprinkled throughout the Bible.

It is difficult to measure how much real evil the false doctrine that was contrived by the Church has loosed on the world. By altering the concept of "The Christ" back in 325 C.E., the Catholic Church has for 1700 years indoctrinated billions of people in a fabricated theology under false religious authority.

All evidence points to the fact that the true Christ is a Divine Principle–an anointing—just as the Gnostics said it was. This is also attested to by any spiritual teaching that taught the pre-Christian esoteric doctrines of the Ancient Wisdom. The "Christ" is a Spiritual Principle, not a human being.

As hard as it may be to swallow today, what the Catholic Church did back in 325 C.E. has for hundreds of years denied people their most precious spiritual birthright–direct access to the Christ Principle as the means of the genuine redemption of their souls.

It makes imminently more sense for The Christ to be a Divine Principle and available to all religions–in fact, any person who actively seeks it, religion or not–rather than a proprietary instrument of one religion, restricted exclusively to those who are members of that religion. Would religious wars be fought over a Divine Principle available to everyone, to *all* religions? The vast cosmos has no room for any exclusivity.

Is it possible to actually think that God, even a Personal God, would chose one "true" church through which the people of the world must evolve spiritually–people He Himself created? Could God be such a bigot?

The world would be much different today if the Roman Catholic Church had just preached the truth early-on. One wonders what it would take today to change our traditional thinking and view all of the religious teachings which have existed since ancient times as a spiritual synthesis, a continuity of progressive spiritual awakenings meant for a particular nation or people in a particular time and place?

Instead we find people believing that the worship of one prophet must be coupled with the disparagement of all others. This is a real divisive measure in the world, but it could be turned around if only the leadership of the churches, temples and mosques could agree that all prophets should be respected. Why can't we look upon all religions and teachings as sequential steps in a spiritual evolution that has been steadily unfolding as surely as our physical evolution? Can we not at least view each religion, each spiritual teaching, as a lustrous pearl in a single necklace of cosmic love emanating from and returning to a non-sectarian Divine Principle?

If there is only One God, why can't that be the God for *all* religions, each different religion realizing that it is but a different method of approach to the same God?

Indeed, why not! Can't we at least follow the lead of the Bible (John 4:24) and explore the possibility of God as an Infinite Spirit? Doesn't it make more sense for all life, all existence, to be a spiritually integrated diversity rather than a hodge-podge of spiritually isolated enclaves?

Can we not at least try to see if there is a common, fundamental oneness underlying all religions and teachings rather than a bunch of Personal-type Gods favoring this or that denomination? And doesn't it make more sense to think of our spiritual future in terms of a new, positive spiritual impetus to coincide with a new evolutionary phase of our spiritual growth than to think that a third of us is going to be lifted up naked to heaven by angels while the other two-thirds burns to death on planet earth!

There is a great need today for a radical change in spiritual consciousness. We need more enlightened, unprejudiced thought if we are to survive as a planet. Therefore it is incumbent upon us to supplant old, unworkable thought patterns with new ways of thinking before those old ways capture and destroy us.

Why can't we embark on an enlightened exploration of all religious concepts in order to discover that which unites, rather than divides, us. Why can't we make a determined study of all the scriptures and pay at least as much attention to allegorical interpretations as we do to the literal wording. That alone could go a long way in getting religions to work together.

It might be a good thing if each of us, regardless of age, could start developing a kind of consciousness of future where the basic paradigm is a unity of diversity where we are unafraid to examine and re-examine all that we have been taught about God, religion and the realm of the spiritual, regardless of by whom or under what authority. Let the different religions be guided by a respect for knowledge, cooperation and tolerance and let all people embrace the concept that science and religion are really after the same things: integrity and truth.

The Lord Buddha told his students, "Believe not what you have heard said; believe not in traditions merely because they have been transmitted through many generations; believe not merely because a thing is repeated by many persons; believe not solely upon the authority of your masters and elders. When upon observation and analysis a principle conforms to reason and leads to the benefit and welfare of all, accept it and hold it."

In other words, let our thinking be based not upon individual prejudices, but upon the concept of what is best for the General Good of all humankind. Not to freely engage in a re-examination and purification of our out-dated dogmatic religious beliefs is to deny us our most precious democratic and constitutional right– freedom of religion.

If we do nothing and fail to re-examine our beliefs as to whether they are fit for the future we will be giving up our hard-won religious independence, handing it over to a body of thought which exists mainly because of its tradition and popularity rather than its integrity.

And what have religions to lose? Do they not have faith in their own dogma; that it can pass the test of unprejudiced investigation and inquiry?

If God is truly an Infinite Spirit, then each person should be able to, through developing their own inner knowledge and understanding of the symbols, myths, metaphors and allegories of creation, gain their own knowledge and experience of God.

Where does it say that we can only experience God through ecclesiastical intercessors? There is no scripture which says we cannot make our own direct connection! And unless religions get wise and take a good hard look at their doctrines and dogma, they will force people to find answers on their own. And the people *will* find them! And the different religions will then have missed out on a great chance to be of real service to spiritual strivers everywhere.

Finally, the most important contribution to a new collective religious consciousness will not be the making of some new religious doctrine. There is nothing wrong with a diversity of approach. In fact, a unity of diversity is the strongest unity known to humankind. Such a unity can be developed by sharing what each of us is able to contribute of our own spiritual thought and experience to a new body of knowledge about God as an infinite, Transcendental Principle. Then we will be free to decide for ourselves what our own truth is. And that truth will be our religion.

As Mme. H. P. Blavatsky so beautifully expressed it, "There is no religion higher than truth."

* * *

Other books by Burt Wilson:

Ancient Wisdom for the 21st Century
Available at www.lulu.com/burtwilson or amazon.com

The Leader (translation) by M. Roerich
Available at www.lulu.com/burtwilson

The Third Theory
Available by e-mail. Contact: bwilson5404@sbcglobal.net

Shakey & Me
Available by e-mail. Contact: bwilson5404@sbcglobal.net

A History of Sacramento Jazz
Available by e-mail. Contact: bwilson5404@sbcglobal.net

Complete Post Production with the Video Toaster
Out of print.

www.ingramcontent.com/pod-product-compliance
Lightning Source LLC
LaVergne TN
LVHW011428080426
835512LV00005B/321